What's Really Going On

A kabbalistic look under
the hood of Creation

Thirtysix.org

What's Really Going On

A Kabbalistic Look Under The Hood of Creation

ISBN 9798353724742

Any questions should be sent to: pinchasw@thirtysix.org.

Published by:
Thirtysix.org
22 Yitzchak Road
Telzstone, Kiryat Yearim
Israel   9083800

in loving memory of my parents

Chaim Leib *ben* **Binyamin Moshe,** *z"l*
Malka *bat* **Avraham,** *z"l*

and my grandparents

Binyamin Moshe *ben* **Avraham Tzvi,** *z"l*
Doris Sarah *bat* **Moshe HaCohen,** *z"l*

Avraham *ben* **Chaim,** *z"l*
Chaya *bat* **Eliezer,** *z"l*

Jonathan Straight
Leeds, England

Introduction

This is not a true story, but it could be. Danny lost his brother at an early age to a rare illness. Only a handful of people have it in any given generation, and Danny's older brother was one of the unfortunate few.

It took only two years for the disease to spread and do its thing, taking Danny's brother's life at the tender age of 16. Danny himself was only 12 at the time, and it hurt him very much. He had felt the helplessness and hopelessness of his family once it became clear that the doctors had no idea how to treat the illness.

Hearing all the wonderful things about his brother at the *shivah* did not help matters. On the contrary, it just made the loss of his older brother that much more painful. On a few occasions, he found himself getting up and going outside to be alone. That's when he would cry and talk to his missing brother.

Shivah became *shloshim*, and the *shloshim* became a year. The *Gemora* says that the heart starts to forget the dead after a year,[1] but Danny's heart seemed to be an exception. Some of the pain had subsided but a lot of it still remained. It concerned his family and friends.

But then Danny realized that it was not his brother he was refusing to let go of. He knew that his brother was in a better place, and felt his presence every time he thought of him. It was as if his brother was still watching over him, as he had always done even into his sickness. It was something else that would not go away.

It was the helplessness. It was that sense of helplessness that he had felt from not being able to help his brother when every part of his being cried out to fix the situation, that wouldn't disappear. And the longer it continued, the more it began to take over his thinking…until one day he found himself saying to himself, "I will find a cure for this horrible disease."

And with those words, a burden was lifted from him, and an unhealthy connection to the past was severed. Even though he was creating a huge life-long challenge for himself, he felt relieved. It made him wonder if his brother

---

[1] *Brochos* 58b.

had anything to do with it from above.

When he shared his decision with his parents, they outwardly admired his resolve while inwardly wondered how long it would last. Until that time, Danny had not particularly excelled in school, and he would have to from that point onward if he wanted to make good on his plans. Becoming a doctor is hard enough. Getting a research grant for a rare disease is almost impossible.

But Danny had already done his research. He was only 14 years old, but he knew how to ask questions. He quickly learned what was involved in his decision, and despite the reservations others had about investing his life in such a focused endeavor, he never wavered. He always had his brother for support.

Overnight his grades improved, slightly at first, and then significantly. He was putting in the time and doing the work, and then some. Every spare moment he had he used to further his personal research into the disease and the means used to research it. For all intents and purposes, he had already started medical school before actually being accepted.

He had gotten used to working hard and being single-minded. It never interfered with his Torah values and obligations, and he felt as if he was doing the work of God. He could not bring back his brother, but at least he could save others from what his brother, and the family, went through. That was a *mitzvah*…a BIG *mitzvah*.

Seven years had not exactly been like one year, but

the time did go by quite quickly. He had graduated with honors and was accepted at several good universities for medicine. He chose the one that he thought would give him the greatest shot at a research grant.

The workload was enormous and the pressure was tremendous, especially to change his mind and focus on other areas of medicine. "You will be a great doctor one day," his professor told him. "Why limit yourself to a very narrow area of medical research?" He would just smile and say, "I'll give it some serious consideration…" knowing full well that he had no plans to veer from his chosen path.

He wrote many grant proposals that came back rejected. So he wrote more grant proposals and they also came back rejected. For the first time in the 15 years since he started thinking about his mission, his will was starting to waver. Did God not want him to succeed? Was his brother unable to pull strings for him above?

He was getting on in life and had to look at the bigger picture. He decided to try one more time, and if that didn't get the desired results, he would look into some other area of practice or research. He had stuck to his guns and done all he could. Now it was Heaven's turn to either support his work or direct him in a different direction.

The board that received the proposal almost voted to reject it. The difference this time was that there was a doctor on the board whose own son had the disease, and he understand Danny's passion to cure it. Soon Danny's passion became his own, and he fought hard to convince the rest of the board to accept the proposal and give the grant.

When the letter from the grant board came in, Danny did not run to open it. He put it neatly to the side of his desk while he went about other business. Part of him wanted to rip the letter open and see the answer, but part of him was afraid to see if decades of work were coming to a premature end. So far, that part was winning.

Finally, when he had a moment, he casually strolled over to his desk and picked up the letter like it was any other as if to make no big deal out of something that was clearly a big deal. He opened the letter and read:

Dear Dr. Weiss,

On behalf of the Board and Trustees of Medical Research, Inc., we are pleased to inform you that your grant proposal to research Disease X has been accepted and is being processed at this time. We hope that this meets with your approval, and we will be sending you another letter shortly with all the details and requirements to activate your grant. We look forward to working with you in the future.

He was shocked. He was so excited that he did not know what to do next. All he could do was fall into his chair and contemplate with excitement what he just read and what it means. He could not wait to get started, but first, he offered a heartfelt prayer of thanks to God, and a promise to do his best to cure the disease. Then he said to his brother, "I know you must have had a hand in this. Thank you, dear brother, and know that I will do my utmost to spare others of what you had to endure."

It took only two years, and the most current technology available to solve the mystery and find a relatively successful drug to fight the disease. It took an additional year and some important collaboration to find a way to effectively deliver the cure to the body so that it could have maximum impact.

Two more years after that the drug had FDA approval and was gaining acceptance around the world. Pharmaceutical companies made the drug available worldwide, and initial results were as good as hoped. In some cases when the drug was used early enough the disease was stopped altogether.

One young child halfway around the world from where Danny did his breakthrough research was about to take his first of many treatments. He was only 10 years old, and his mother handed him the pill with trepidation. Would it work? Would it make him worse? Would the side effects be miserable?

As the boy placed the pill into his mouth and drank water to wash it down and let it begin its work, he had no idea that he was swallowing the will of a 12-year-old boy named Danny Weiss who lived somewhere in America. He did not know that the cure he was ingesting was really the desire of another young boy, now all grown up with a family of his own, to cure people with the disease his own brother suffered from.

But that's what it was. The pill casing was just the *physical* means of delivery for the *physical* cure inside. But the *physical* cure inside was just the *physical* actualization of the *spiritual* will that made it possible. If he could have, Danny Weiss would have just *willed* everyone with his brother's disease to be instantly cured. But not being able to do that, he was more than happy to have discovered a physical means to accomplish the same thing.

And so was God, as the next chapter explains.

Means of Delivery

The topic of will is fascinating. It is such an abstract reality that can have such incredibly non-abstract results. A person can make a single decision and change the whole world. President Truman must have had tremendous reservations about dropping the bomb on Japan, but at one point he decided to do it and changed the course of history.

What is it, this whole will thing?

It seems to start with a *want* that somehow evolves into a *need* which then evolves into a *desire* to have or do. It is this desire that sets some process in motion that has the express aim of fulfilling that desire in an acceptable manner.

For example, a person may become thirsty. This will create a want to quench the thirst, and then a desire for drink. This desire will cause the person to consider where to find water, and if they find some, they will have *will* to get some of it. Once they do this, their body will go through the necessary motions to acquire it, drink it, and stop the thirst.

Will is *everything*. Nothing gets done without it. A person does not get out of bed in the morning without the will to do so. Without blood, we die, but we take that for granted. Without will we also die, and also take that for granted.

Until, that is, it gets thwarted. The most frustrating thing in life is having the will for something and no means to fulfill it. It can cause people to lose it, and in some cases, cause some to give up on everything including life itself. We overlook it while we have it, and go crazy once we lose it, even if only because of ourselves.[1] Go figure.

Our will is amazing and worth a much longer discussion. But if you want to appreciate the amazing power of will, consider God's. Everything that exists and everything that survives is all a function of His will every single second of its existence and survival. Us too.

As the *Nefesh HaChaim* explains in the first *sha'ar*, it takes will for man to create something, but once it exists his

---

[1] Sometimes people want to try something, but personal fears or laziness constantly prevent them from doing what they will.

will is no longer necessary to maintain it. It takes will to build a house, but once built the house will remain standing even after the builder has left. But once God withdraws His will, whatever He created ceases to exist immediately. His will is the lifeforce of all existence.

Another fundamental difference between the will of God and the will of man is that man is limited in the execution of his will. Not everything man wills can he fulfill. Not God though. His will is infinite and He can infinitely fulfill it at any time he chooses.

So for example, if God wanted to create a being that will eventually go to the World-to-Come and be rewarded for lifetimes of moral choices, He can put that being in the World-to-Come from the start. He can give that being a sense of having lived many lives and made many choices, even though they didn't. All He would have to do is will it, and it would be.

But that's not the way He did it. Instead, God created an entire world that can create its own history and its own future. People live and experience life, allowing them to make choices that impact their lives and the world. All of it can never be different from the will of God, but that does not stop the world from going through all that it does. It's all the will of God.

How does that work? How does the will of God get translated into things that exist and things that occur? What is the "pill" that God created to deliver His will to its intended destination to have its intended impact? And how does it translate from something completely abstract to something tangible?

The short answer? The *sefiros*. The Hebrew word *l'sapper* means *to count* because each *sefirah* is a quantifiable amount of divine light, divinely designed to execute the will of God in a very specific way on a very specific level. They are God's chosen *means of delivery* of His will for Creation and history.

None of the *sefiros* are physical, not even on the level responsible for the physical world. They are completely *spiritual* entities, spiritual vessels containing spiritual light. And even though the vessels are to their light what our physical bodies are to our spiritual souls, they are still *completely* spiritual. Welcome to the miracle of life.

The technical term for that miracle is *Yaish m'Ayin*— *something from nothing*. We don't know how it works, just that it works, or we wouldn't be here. We might be able to understand the idea somewhat if we had a better grasp of *Ayin* (not going to happen), or even just of *Yaish*, which even scientists are finding out is not as obvious as we previously assumed.

Imagine 10 balls spread out over a length of rope, held tautly at both ends by different people. If one person decides to shake the rope at their end, their moving of the first ball will cause the second ball to move, then the third, etc., all the way down the rope until the tenth ball moves in the other person's hand.

Physically, it was the up-and-down movement that

set off a chain reaction that moved from ball to ball down the rope. *Metaphysically*, it was the *will* of the first person that got everything moving, and what travelled down the rope through the motion. The motion just carried the will of the first person to the second person.

The stating point of all of Creation is that God *willed* to be revealed. Nothing existed at that time but the will of God to be revealed and known by another, and that translated into creating a means to share His light. That, in turn, resulted in the Creation of a contained reality called the *Challal*—Hollow, and a being within the *Challal* with whom God could share His light, us, of course.[2]

It's like a person who has an idea that they wish to convey to others. Therefore, they write a play to be acted out to deliver their message to an audience. But this necessitates a playhouse and stage, which they build as well, and after everything is constructed and in place, they open the doors to the audience. At the end of the play, the message has been revealed to the audience.

To be successful, the writer had to custom-design the playhouse to enable their message to get across. If you took a tour of the place, you'd be absolutely amazed at what you would see, details upon details upon details. Even things that were built for aesthetics only were added as part

---

[2] All of the information presented here is found in many primary *kabbalistic* works, especially the *Aitz Chaim* of the *Arizal*. *Otzros Chaim*, a more condensed version, begins with this discussion.

of the viewing experience, to help the message make its mark.

Even a simple broom closet is part of the experience. For the play to be a success the set has to be swept clean each day. That requires a broom, and the broom requires a closet, to keep it from sight and from getting lost. Every last thing…every last screw…every last nail…every last minutiae, visible or invisible, is part of the execution of the will of the playwright.

The audience may have asked, "What is the purpose of all this?" when they first sat down. But by the time the play was over they understood very well why all of it was brought into being, and why they were invited to experience it all.

When people ask, "What is the purpose of life?" they are really asking, "What is the will of God?" They are one and the same question. And though you do not need to be religious to ask either, you do need to believe in a creator to appreciate the answer. Not believing in a *willful* origin of life is like believing a play randomly wrote itself. It might be entertaining but it certainly isn't very meaningful.

Part of the unfathomable will of God is how He made everything—from the teensy little physical world that we call massive, to all the massive spiritual worlds above it that most people do not even know about—just to reveal Himself to man. To reveal themself to another, a person need only introduce themself without any fanfare. To reveal Himself to man, God created the *Challal* and everything in it.

What is the *Challal*? It is the divine playhouse, if you will. It is the stage that God created to allow His will to be acted out before others so that they can independently know that God exists. For the moment, it is just the shell into which everything else will be built, including human beings.

If a playwright does not build a theater, they could always have their play performed in the streets. It might be less than ideal, but it is doable. But without a *Challal*, revelation to another is not doable, because all that would exist is God's infinite light infinitely in every direction. Nothing else other than the light of God can exist in such a situation. To reveal Himself he "had" to build the playhouse.

Therefore, God willed *tzimtzum* on Himself and constricted His light. This, of course, is the biggest oxymoron ever because His infinite light remained infinite even though a relatively very small circular area in the "center" of His infinite light—the *Challal*—did not, at least not in any noticeable way. It was like a very, very huge basketball filled up with air, except that outside *this* "ball" was infinite light held out only by the will of God, not some kind of non-porous rubber skin.

It was the first level of *Yaish m'Ayin*, but still a long way from being the place a person can live and become aware of God. Not even angels can exist on this level. That would take additional *tzimtzum,* this time inside the *Challal* itself.

But *tzimtzum* of what? If the Infinite Light was being kept at bay on the outside of the *Challal*, what was left on the inside of the *Challal* to constrict?

Ohr Ain Sof, God's infinite light.

Where did it come from?

From the outside.

How did it get in again, and why did it not obliterate the *Challal*?

Because this time it came into the *Challal* in a limited amount, what is called the *Kav Ain Sof*—Line (of Light) Without End. The biggest oxymoron ever continued into the *Challal* with a thin line of infinite light, like this:

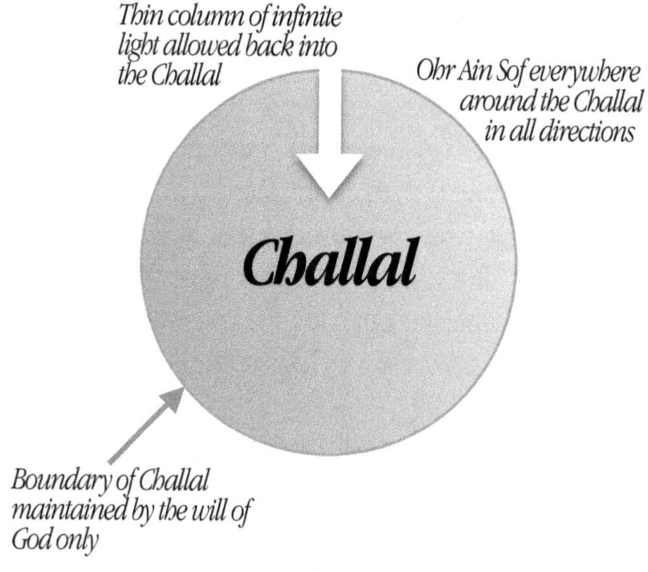

It's like building a skyscraper. First a massive hole is dug in the ground for the foundation, the *challal*. Then materials are dropped off at the site which will be used to construct the building, level by level from the foundation up. The *Kav Ain Sof* was, is, the "material" required to allow Creation to actualize the original will of God. Though the light is sublimely spiritual, it contains the potential for all that will ever exist, spiritual *and* physical.

Unlike electricity which gets weaker with distance, the *Ohr Ain Sof* can continue forever without losing any of its infinite intensity. It doesn't have to deal with any kind of resistance like an electrical current does, other than the will of God, that it become less intense. He created the 10 completely spiritual *sefiros* to create that resistance and weaken the intensity of His light.

A *sefirah* is a filter. It receives divine light which, as it passes through the *sefirah* on its way to lower levels, is filtered. The body of the *sefirah* is able to hold back certain aspects of the light it receives, which becomes its own soul so-to-speak, allowing the remainder of the light to continue on down to the next *sefirah* and level…all according to the very specific will of God.

Right after the *Ohr Ain Sof* re-entered the *Challal* as the *Kav*, it manufactured a vessel called *Keser*—Crown, since it sits on top of the system like a crown on a head. That's the simple explanation for the name, but it is enough for now.

The wall of the vessel has thickness, having an inside,

middle, and outside, as per the will of God. Some of the light of the *Kav* remains only light and within the vessel, like a soul in a body, while the rest of the light continues on down. Together, the vessel of *Keser* and the light within it are the *sefirah* called *Keser*.

The next level is called *Chochmah*—Wisdom. The light on the level of *Keser* is so abstract that it is completely ungraspable to man. As God told Moshe *Rabbeinu* who requested a glimpse of such knowledge:

> *"You will not be able to see My face, for man shall not see Me and live."* (*Shemos* 33:20)

God of course has no face, and no one can see Him, period. Face here is a euphemism for a very direct and intense level of light,[3] exposure to which would kill a person.[4] Moshe wanted to know the will of God on the most primordial of levels, but was denied since he could not have survived it.[5]

On the level of *Chochmah,* the light/knowledge is still very abstract, but somewhat graspable. We can see some of it by opening the *Zohar* and *Arizal* that speak

---

[3] Just as a face is a direct revelation of a person versus the back of the head.

[4] The body cannot handle that high a level of divine light.

[5] *Sha'ar HaGilgulim,* Introduction 28; *Drushei Olam HaTohu, Chelek 2, Drush 4, Anaf 14, Siman 1-2.*

about the origins of Creation. Most people may not be able to grasp the full meaning of what is written on such levels of Torah (and we don't even have all of it), but they can at least be made aware of them. This is the level of *Sod*,[6] the highest level of Torah learning we know of.

The light is filtered again in the process of making the *sefirah* of *Chochmah*, and results in the next level of *sefirah* called *Binah*—Understanding. On this level, the knowledge revealed through the light is far less abstract, more down-to-earth. It can be understood in terms of Creation and everyday life as we know it.

The change from *Chochmah* to *Binah* is fundamentally *Yaish m'Ayin*. *Chochmah* is a completely spiritual and godly level. *Binah* is the beginning of *Ma'aseh Bereishis*—physical Creation, and though *Binah* is still quite high up in the system, it is more closely connected to the lower worlds than the ones above it.[7]

This level corresponds to the level of *Drush*, exegesis, like the *Gemora*, for example. Unlike *Kabbalah*, which is completely abstract and discusses nothing about the everyday world we live in, *Gemora* only deals with our world and how to *halachically* navigate life.

On this level of Torah, the light of *Chochmah* is hid-

---

[6] Literally, *secret*, but it refers specifically to *Kabbalah*.

[7] This is even though *Binah* has been "paired" with *Chochmah* "face-to-face" ever since *Tikun Ma'aseh Bereishis*.

den from us, clothed in worldly matters.[8] The same rabbis who are featured in the *Gemora* were also the greatest *kabbalists* of their time, though you wouldn't know this from how they speak there. But the lack of *kabbalistic* abstractness is specifically what makes the light/knowledge/will of God on the level of *Binah* understandable.

Another name for *Keser, Chochmah,* and *Binah* is *mochin*—brains. This is because the actual set up of the *sefiros, function-wise,* is like a human being, with a head, torso, legs, etc. This makes the top three *sefiros* like the head of the system, sharing with Creation the "thinking" of God, in a manner-of-speaking.

The next six *sefiros* of *Chesed, Gevurah, Tifferes, Netzach, Hod,* and *Yesod,* which correspond to the *body* of the system, teach us more about how God acts in Creation. They are the will of God in action. The light of *Binah* filtered results in the *sefirah* of *Chesed*—Kindness, something that Avraham *Avinu* came to exemplify after *understanding* his Creator.

Chesed is the foundation of Creation, as it says:

Forever will it be built with kindness. (Tehillim 89:3)

Therefore, this *sefirah* is represented by Avraham *Avinu* whose *chassadim* was legendary. He exemplified the trait of *Chesed* because he came to understand how

---

[8] *Drushei Olam HaTohu, Chelek 1, Drush 5, Siman 7, Os 8.*

important it is to God. For this reason he was called a *merkavah*—chariot for the *Shechinah*,[9] because everywhere Avraham went it was as if God rode with him.

The *Midrash* says:

And God said, "Let there be light!" (Bereishis 1:3)— This refers to Avraham. (*Bereishis Rabbah* 2:3)

When God commanded the light into existence, it was not the physical light with which we are accustomed. He ordered the *Ohr Ain Sof,* the light of His will, to penetrate deeper into the *Challal* and bring light to the darkness, to actualize the potential for life and His reason for Creation.

Equating Avraham *Avinu* with this light meant that his existence, his life, was the physical manifestation of this sublime light and will. The light didn't just give Avraham life and potential as it does all of us. It directed him, flowed through him into the world as it does through the *sefiros*…and to his son and spiritual heir, *Yitzchak.*

Gevurah is the exact opposite of *Chesed.* Filtering the light on the level of *Chesed* should result in a next level that is just less *Chesed,* not the *opposite* of it. That would imply that all the light was held back, which could not have been the case since there were still five more *sefiros* left to create, some of which would be *Chesed*-based.

---

9 *Bereishis Rabbah* 47:6.

The truth is, we have all experienced this dilemma in life. A parent loves to give to their child and make them happy. But sometimes circumstances make giving the wrong thing to do because, any giving that is not for the ultimate good of the recipient is no giving at all. There are times when holding back and denial is the greater and more meaningful gift.

Or in the case of Avraham, slaughtering his beloved son on the command of God. It was the fine tuning of his *chesed*, showing Avraham that just as water, to which *chesed* is compared, requires the *gevurah* of a glass to make it easier to drink, likewise unbridled *chesed* can be more damaging than good. *Chesed* is not only about giving. It is primarily about *thoughtful* and *disciplined* giving, to ourselves and others.

Therefore, even though *Gevurah* can result in strict justice and discipline, since it is for the ultimate good of the recipient, it is still *chesed*. It is *gemilus*[10] *chassadim*, *chesed* designed to promote a person's independence and personal godliness.

Creation was the result of *tzimtzum*, which means boundaries and measurement. But *tzimtzum* without a flow of light, like the *Kav Ain Sof*, means nothing, results in

---

[10] This comes from the same word for camel, *gamal*, which can go for days without water in the desert, making it more independent than other animals. It is also the same root of the word for weaning—*gemilah*—because it makes the child more independent.

nothing. It is the working together of *Chesed* and *Gevurah* that makes everything possible, and the balance of which results in beautiful harmony, or the *sefirah* of *Tifferes*, represented by Ya'akov *Avinu* and the source of Torah.

Life is a dichotomy. It is a mixture of two opposite forces, *chesed* and *gevurah*. Mistakes occur when someone mistakenly acts with too much of one or the other. Shaul's misplaced mercy on the king of Amalek allowed the greatest threat to mankind to continue until this day. Elisha's rejection of his right-hand man, *Gechazi*, caused him to turn his back on God and Torah. Tragically, history is full of examples of both, and the terrible destruction they caused.

Mastering life as God meant it to be mastered means finding the right balance of both *chesed* and *gevurah* in any given situation throughout all of life. This is what Avraham and Yitzchak learned through their tests, and that knowledge was embodied in the third of the *Avos*, Ya'akov *Avinu*, whose life began in the tents of Torah.

Torah is the only way to find that balance in life. This is why Torah law is called *halachah* from the word *holech—walk*. Life is a journey, and Torah is our most reliable guide for walking it meaningfully. Otherwise, life is purely guesswork, based purely on trial-and-error. The fact that psychiatry is one of the most lucrative professions says that we're not so good at figuring out life that way.

Filtering *Tifferes* results in the *sefirah* of *Netzach*, which can mean *victory, dominance,* and *eternal.* It is also said to be one of the two sources of prophecy, the other being the next *sefirah* of *Hod*. Therefore, *Netzach* corresponds to Moshe *Rabbeinu*, the greatest prophet to have ever lived, and who was all of these things.

Moshe *Rabbeinu* exemplified this trait of God, just as the *Avos* before him did the traits at which they excelled. When a person acts like Moshe *Rabbeinu*, it means they think in terms of eternity, what ultimately counts, not what only matters in the short run. It means they are a warrior for God and His truth.

But when a person acts like Aharon *HaKohen*, Moshe *Rabbeinu's* brother,[11] they are emulating a different trait: the glory of being made in the image of God. Everyone does this to some degree, but the *kehunah* was devoted to this trait to the exclusion of all else, and Aharon *HaKohen* the most of everyone. This is the *sefirah* of *Hod*—Glory.

The *omer*[12] is counted for 49 days between the second night of *Pesach* and *Shavuos*. The forty-nine days are

---

[11] The *Zohar* (*Acharei* 57b) refers to *Netzach* and *Hod* as two halves of a single body.

[12] On the evening after the first day of Pesach, three men would reap three *se'ah* of barley. After, they brought the barley to the Temple courtyard where they thrashed, winnowed, and roasted the kernels. The kernels were spread out in the Temple courtyard and the wind wafted through it. After, the barley was ground to produce three *se'ah*, and after it had been sifted with 13 sifters, an *issaron* was removed mixed with oil and frankincense. It was waved in the eastern portion of the Temple courtyard in all four directions, etc. Without the Temple, we merely count the days of the *omer* each day starting the second night of *Pesach* and finishing the night before *Shavuos*.

divided into two periods, the first 32 days of the *Omer*, the gematria of *leiv*—heart, and the last 17 days, the *gematria* of *tov*—good. The day that separates the two periods and acts as a threshold from *leiv* to *leiv tov* is *Lag B'Omer,* the 33rd day of the *Omer*. It was the day that Rebi Shimon *bar* Yochai revealed the *Zohar* to his *talmidim, Hod Sh'b'Hod* in the *sefiros.*

Tradition teaches that the seven weeks of the *Omer* correspond to the seven *sefiros* of *Chesed* through *Malchus,* which have their own seven *sefiros* with the same names.[13] *Hod* corresponds to the fifth week of the *Omer* Count, and the 33rd day of the *Omer* is the fifth day within *Hod*, which is also *Hod*. Hence, *Hod Sh'b'Hod*, the glory within glory, and the revelation of the hidden glory of Torah, *Kabbalah*.

Yesod means *foundation* and is associated with right-eousness, as it says:

The righteous person is the foundation of the world. (*Mishlei* 10:25)

It is the *sefirah* of Yosef *HaTzaddik* who earned his title by rejecting the sexual advances of his master's wife.[14] This is not incidental since *Yesod* corresponds to the male

---

[13] Each actually has all ten *sefiros*, but for this level of *tikun* only the bottom seven are considered.

[14] *Bereishis* 39:12.

sexual organ on which the Jewish people perform *Bris Milah* and reaffirm the covenant made with Avraham *Avinu*.

Until the *Yesod*, the divine light and will traveled internally from *sefirah* to *sefirah*, creating all that it did. Both were revealed through what was created, which is why Avraham Avinu was able to discern the reality before receiving prophecy. He just reverse-engineered Creation to become aware of the will that created all of it. Every building is just the three-dimensional expression of its blueprint.

The same is true for the seed that travels through a man to create a child. It travels internally through the man until the *Yesod*, at which time it leaves the *Yesod* for the world beyond it. In the case of a human seed, it is the woman who will gestate the seed and bear the child. In the case of divine light, it is the revelation of truth through education. In the case of Yosef *HaTzaddik*, it was all of this, as well as the sustenance he provided the world as viceroy of Egypt.

Thus, the *Arizal* says that good teachers are usually rooted in the *sefirah* of *Yesod* on some level.[15] The Torah that comes from their mouths is the divine light that emanates to the outside world through some means of teaching.

Yesod is also associated with redemption for the same reason, which is why there is a *Moshiach Ben Yosef*. Redemption is really just the revelation of God's light less

---

[15] *Sha'ar HaGilgulim.*

filtered, causing miracles to occur and evil to weaken, and that is a Yosef-like role, as even Pharaoh acknowledged:

So Pharaoh said to his servants, "Will we find [any- one] like this, a man in whom there is the spirit of God?" (Bereishis 41:38)

Eventually, the revelation of divine light will be so intense and continuous that evil will be completely and eternally eradicated, as the verse says:

God will be King over the entire land. On that day, God will be One and His Name will be One. (Zechariah 14:9)

Therefore, when God declared war against Amalek at the end of *Parashas Beshallach*, He declared it against the main source of blockage. As *Rashi* explains there, Amalek divides God's Name, between the *Yud-Heh* and *Vav-Heh*, the name which corresponds to *Zehr Anpin*, the body of sefiros from *Chesed* to *Yesod*.

Amalek uses doubt, which is why his name is equal in *gematria* to *suffek*—doubt. Intellectual clarity is the result of receiving divine light. Doubt is the result of not receiving enough of it, which is what happens to people who do not know what it is or why it is important to access it.

This is also why it is *Moshiach Ben Yosef* who battles

and defeats Amalek.[16] A *tzaddik* is the foundation of Creation because he is the conduit for the light and will of God, banishing intellectual darkness and doubt from the world, ending the reign of Amalek:

> *God said, "My spirit that is upon you and My words that I have placed in your mouth." (Yeshayahu 59:20)*

Yesod is the ninth *sefirah* in the overall system, which means the light has been filtered *eight* times since leaving *Keser*. Like a prism reveals the different colors of the spectrum as the light passes through it, the *sefiros* revealed the different *middos* of God's will as His light passed through them.

After so much filtering, what was left for the *Malchus*, the tenth and final *sefirah*? No wonder it came out with so few *sefiros* of its own. But isn't the *Malchus* the endgame? Isn't it what we are trying to build down here in the world of man, *Malchus Shamayim*, the Kingdom of Heaven? This is why *Malchus* deserves a chapter of its own.

---

[16] *Rashi, Bereishis 30:25; Shem M'Shmuel, Parashas Vayishlach.*

Building *Malchus*

*I*t is interesting how any group of people that live together eventually form a
malchus—kingdom. Even tribes that grow
up away from any forms of western culture
that might influence their thinking end with some form of
malchus. Someone will invariably rise to the top and become a king-like figure, and everyone else will end up being their subjects. It seems to be one of the most natural
societal processes there are.

It seems to evolve out of common need. There is
safety in numbers. There is greater success in numbers.
There is companionship in numbers. And without some
form of leadership, the numbers usually do not function to
capacity, if at all. A king needs a kingdom and a kingdom

needs a king.

It's a reflection of Heaven. Heaven is a kingdom as well, and God is King. And since we are told that God only made all of it to give us the very best good possible, being King over His kingdom must somehow be for our good. So much so, in fact, that we accept upon ourselves the yoke of the Kingdom of Heaven twice a day by saying the *Shema*.

If you think about it, the idea of *malchus* is part-and-parcel with Creation. A *malchus* bands together many individuals into a single whole without compromising their individuality. Any personal sacrifices made are for the good of the whole, which in turn benefits the individuals.

Since God is everywhere and everything is a part of Him, He is by definition a *malchus, the Malchus*. We are banded together by His all-pervasive reality which encompasses everything, and yet we nevertheless remain individuals. The *Ohr Ain Sof* means that nothing can be separate from God, and yet *tzimtzum* means that somehow we can live as if we are. It's just another way of describing the miracle of life.

Our bodies are also an expression of *malchus*. We are a conglomerate of countless parts, large and small, working individually and in synchrony for the sake of the whole, *us*. The brain is king orchestrating all of it, unless our will enters the picture and overrides the brain, telling it what to do.

Just about anywhere you look, *malchus* is at work, synergizing various different components into a confluent whole. This is true on a microscopic level, or on a grand scale such as the solar system with eight planets[1] circling king sun. It's basically *malchus* everywhere in Creation.

It can be, and is, very deceiving. Look how many people over the ages have failed to notice God. And becoming smarter hasn't helped. Scientists are some of the intellectual elite of secular society, and they look God in the face and still can't see Him. Amalek makes sure of that.

The goal is to change that:

Here O Israel, the Lord our God, the Lord is One. (Devarim 6:4)

God, who is now *our* God and not the God of the other nations, will be declared in the future "the one God," as it says: *"For then I will convert the peoples to a pure language that all of them call in the name of God"* (Tzephaniah 3:9), and, *"On that day, God will be One and His Name will be One"* (Zechariah 14:9). (*Rashi*)

It's just a question of bringing enough light down from *Yesod* to *Malchus*. A certain amount of light comes down anyhow just to maintain Creation independent of the actions of man. But God left it for man to bring additional light down to transform all the earthly *malchiyos* into

---

[1] Pluto has been downgraded to a dwarf planet.

Malchus Shamayim on earth.

This is the idea of *Kiddush Hashem*, the sanctification of the Name of God. It is a Torah *mitzvah* for a Jew to sanctify the Name of God, which means performing *mitzvos* in a way that draws additional divine light/will into the world of *Malchus*. It is the most meaningful thing a person can do, and the basis of their reward in the World-to-Come.

Dovid *HaMelech* is associated with this trait, and *Tehillim* is a good example of why. It makes perfectly clear that God runs the world, and that everything is a function of *hashgochah pratis*, divine providence. And it emphasizes that everything that happens to us is for our ultimate good, something only God can guarantee.

Moshiach Ben Dovid will do on a world level in our time what Dovid *HaMelech* did for only the Jewish people in his time. He will bring about the fulfillment of the verses from Tzephaniah and Zechariah through his very existence, and because of all the miracles he will perform en route to the final redemption. That is the *Malchus Shamayim* on earth.

When that happens then a major change will occur. The *Malchus* will finally be built and complete, and will ascend as high as *Binah,* and elevate all the *sefiros* in-between. Our world that, for thousands of years since the sin of the *Aitz HaDa'as Tov v'Ra,* has been embedded in the *Klipos,* will finally leave them.

In fact, the *Klipos* will no longer exist because all evil

will be gone from Creation.[2] All the sparks will have become removed from them, denying them further sustenance and they will disappear like smoke. The *yetzer hara* will be history,[3] and any truly evil people who did not merit to live into the Messianic Era. The reality of God will be palpable like never before.

It will be like a king who lost his throne and later regained it with all its glory. It came from *Keser*, was "banished" to the lowest parts of the Creation to fulfill the needs of history, and eventually reascended to its rightful place from the Messianic time on.[4]

But as the *Gemora* explains, there are two times that this can happen, early—*achishenah*—or at the last possible moment—*b'ittah*.[5] That is, we can complete the will of God for this stage of history early, or we can wait for the will of God to complete itself.

The difference between the two endings? The *Gemora* answers that as well. Early means a peaceful transition to *Yemos HaMoshiach*, and last moment means a major war, what the prophets and later rabbis called the War of Gog and Magog. We are no strangers to world wars, but not to one like this:

---

[2] *Sha'ar HaGilgulim*, Introduction 20.

[3] *Succah* 52a.

[4] Very much like what actually happened to Dovid *HaMelech* and later his son, Shlomo *HaMelech*.

[5] *Sanhedrin* 98a.

A time of trouble such as has never been seen.
(*Daniel* 12:1)

*Behold, a day of God comes, when your spoil shall
be divided in your midst. For I will gather all nations against Jerusalem to battle; and the city shall
be taken, and the houses rifled, and the women rav-
ished; and half of the city will go into captivity, but
the rest of the people will not be cut off from the
city...* (*Zechariah* 14:1-2)

The war will draw down whatever light needs to be
drawn down to end history and begin the Messianic Era.
Achishenah would mean that we did that on our own
through the learning of Torah and the performance of
mitzvos. B'ittah means we didn't, and the War of Gog and
Magog, whatever it is and whomever it involves, will make
up for the shortfall.

How? That remains to be seen, but the *Gemora* does
say this:

It has been taught: Ben Zoma asked the rabbis, "Will
the exodus from Egypt be mentioned in the days of
Moshiach? Was it not said long ago, 'Therefore, behold days are coming, says God, when they shall no
longer say, *"As God lives, Who brought up the Children of Israel from the land of Egypt,"* but, *"As God
lives, Who brought up and Who brought the seed of*

*the House of Israel from the northland and from all
the lands where I have driven them, and they shall
dwell on their land" (Yirmiyahu 23:7-8)' ?"*

They answered, "This does not mean that the mention of the exodus from Egypt will be eliminated, but that the [redemption from] the oppression of other kingdoms will become primary and the exodus from Egypt will become secondary." (*Brochos* 12b)

It's simple. Pharaoh asked, *"Who is God that I should heed His voice to let Israel out?"*[6] The Ten Plagues answered his question and he ended up letting the Jewish people out. Later, he thought that it was his god trapping the Jewish people by the sea. God left no doubt when He drowned Pharaoh's entire army while Pharaoh watched in horror from the side.

We've come a long way since *Yetzias Mitzrayim*. It's a far more technologically advanced society. We fight more technologically sophisticated wars and watch movies that take the world's imagination even further. It would take a lot to convince the world in our time what it took 10 plagues to convince Pharaoh of in his time. And that will be the War of Gog and Magog.

If, that is, we do not bring that light down on our own before it is too late. That light, and so much more of it, is waiting in the *sefiros* from *Keser* to *Hod*, to be brought

---

[6] *Shemos* 5:2.

down to the *sefirah* of *Malchus* and rectify the world. We just have to turn the valve, which is *Yesod*, and let the light flow into the world in sufficient abundance.

Over time, that would not be so hard if enough people are learning Torah and performing *mitzvos*, each with the proper intention. The persecution and the wars of the past is what Jewish and world history look like when more light needs to be in the world than has been brought down in time, what the *Gemora* calls a *keitz*—end time.[7]

They don't happen suddenly. There are signs. There are warnings. There always are in any *malchus* that is not functioning as it should. But there is also ignorance and misinterpretation, which renders the signs and warnings meaningless, except for a few who understand them correctly but are powerless to do enough about them on their own. Perhaps the Holocaust could have been worse, but it was already *horribly* bad.

Think of the *Malchus* as an almost empty pitcher, and the *Yesod* as a faucet from which the *Malchus* can be filled to capacity with divine light. The other eight *sefiros* above *Yesod* are like the pipe in the wall that brings the water, or in this case, the light from its source—the *Ohr Ain Sof*—to the faucet. It's all there, the entire system, and more rectifying light than we could ever imagine…if only someone would open the faucet.

To understand what this means and how to do it, we

---

[7] *Sanhedrin* 97b.

have to look at little more deeply at the *sefiros* and how they work. Amazingly, we have examples of this all around us in our world. What we lack is the understanding that this is what we are looking at, and what we must utilize if we are to fulfill the will of God peacefully.

Male & Female

hough Adam was created first, Chava was not too far behind. God did not create a second man, with whom the first man could build the world and share experiences. God created a female, took her right from within man, and then married them to each other. The creation of the next man was the result of their relationship.

Historically, some have tried *unnaturally* to break the *natural* rules, but it never matches the sublime simplicity of the God-given system. And though they like to say that the system is more a function of *nurture* than *nature*, the facts speak for themselves clearly, as clearly as the sun rising each day in the east and setting in the west.

Part of the difference of opinion has to do with the understanding of such relationships. Is there an actual *mitzvah* to get married? Not really. There is a *mitzvah* for a man to try to have children, and that necessitates a holy relationship called marriage, which necessitates *kiddushin* and *nesu'in*, what might be called engagement and actual marriage.[1]

God could have made the world any way He wanted, and it would have worked. It could have been a world of all men or all women, and He still could have made it that propagation of the species was still possible. With God, the sky is not the limit. Infinity is.

But He didn't. He decided in His infinite and unfathomable wisdom to make a male component and a female component, and to bring them together to create children. This started in *Gan Aiden*, in the Garden of Eden, and it continues until this very day.

The truth is, the male and female relationship predated the creation of man and woman, even of the world. In fact, one of the main *tikunim* long before *Ma'aseh Bereishis* was the separation of the male and female components into separate entities.[2] From that point onward,

---

[1] Unlike engagement in the secular world, for all *halachic* intents and purposes *kiddushin* is marriage. It would require a *get* and divorce to end it, which is why the rabbis pushed *kiddushin* off until the actual day of the *chuppah*, which is what *halachically* permits a man and woman to live together in seclusion.

[2] *Biur HaGR"A, Sifra D'Tzniusa*, Ch. 1.

there were male *sefiros* and female *sefiros*, the former being the side of *Chesed* in the *sefiros* and the latter, the side of *Gevurah*.

This was essential to the process of creation because existing lights had to give rise to new lights, and this, basically, is the result of something called *zivug*, the *pairing* of male *sefiros* with female *sefiros*, like *Chochmah* with *Binah*, and lower down, *Zehr Anpin* (*Chesed* through *Yesod*) with *Nukvah* (*Malchus*).

As to *why* God did it this way, we don't know. We just know that He did, and that this is the very best way to make the world, or He would have made it differently. A fundamental of Creation is that God is *perfect* and only gives the *perfect* good,[3] no matter how *imperfect* it may seem to us at this time.

In the Torah world, only when a man and woman reach the age of marriage do they begin dating, and only for that purpose. If they find themselves compatible spiritual and physically, they decide to get married and begin raising a family. There is no such thing a pre-marital relationship, and children are certainly not born outside of marriage.

As backwards as this may sound to a secular person today, it is the way of the world, including up in the *sefiros*. Life is the result of divine light flowing down into our world, and that light is the result of *zivugim*, the pairing of

---

[3] *Derech Hashem*, The Purpose of Creation.

specific *sefiros* at specific times to produce specific lights. And *kabbalistically*, they are all male-female, husband-wife relationships.

As mentioned, one of the main *zivugim* is between the *sefiros* of *Chochmah* and *Binah*, otherwise known as *Abba* and *Imma*—Father and Mother. The lower down pairing that we actually impact with our choices and actions is between *Zehr Anpin* and *Nukvah* in general, and various different versions of this *zivug* that occur during different parts of day and night.

A person in need knows to pray to God for help. What they usually do not know is that they are trying to create some kind of *zivug* on some level to have their request fulfilled. They might be praying for money, or health, to find their soul mate, etc. Whatever they lack is only going to materialize if it first originates as a light "born" as a result of a *zivug* triggered by their prayer.

Or by their *mitzvah*. The better the *mitzvah* performed, the greater the likelihood of a *zivug* that can give birth to a light that will bring them *brochah*—blessing. Because just as a baby is born as a result of a pairing between husband and wife, resulting in something very small that gestates and becomes something bigger, so too does the light of a *zivug* in the *sefiros*.

And just as a fetus grows to become an independent life before it is born, likewise does the light of our blessing begin as a single light that grows into its own complement of ten lights until it becomes an independent *sefirah*. Then it is born and shows up in the physical world as the blessing we need, sometimes without even asking for it.

Under 400,000 babies are born a day in the world, a lot less than the amount of lights born into the world from the pairing of *sefiros*. Many *sefiros* "births" happen automatically, having little to actually to do with man, otherwise the world could not survive even minimally. We just don't do enough to keep the world going.

But sometimes we elevate so few sparks, which we will see is essential for the pairing process, that even what happens automatically is not enough to justify Creation. This is what led to the martyrdom of the 10 great rabbis mentioned in the repetition of the *Yom Kippur Mussaf*. Their heroic deaths and sanctification of God's Name compensated for what was lacking to keep Creation going.[4]

Others *sefiros* have been left for man to cause into existence, so that we can participate in the rectification of the world and be rewarded for it. Unbeknownst to most of us, this is what we are doing everyday just by getting up in the morning and accomplishing things before going to bed at night. Just *what* we accomplish determines what we create, and how much of it.

How does it work?

That's like asking how digestion works. You can answer, "You eat, you swallow, and you digest," which is 100 percent true. It just leaves out a lot of very important steps

---

4 *Aitz Chaim, Sha'ar HaKlallim, Klal* 2.

in-between that are crucial for making sure the system works the way it should.

Likewise, we could answer, "You do a *mitzvah*, sparks go up, and you make a *sefirah*," but again, so many important details are being ignored. And they are details that make a difference to everything we do and how we do it, not to mention our portions in the World-to-Come.

It would be great to start from the very beginning, at least as we know it. But that will take too long and provide too much information, so we'll start in the middle where it affects us the most and where we are the most effective, the creation of our world.

The world we can see is amazing. The world we can't see is even more amazing. If we could see it, our lives would never be the same again. Books and movies have tried to imagine it, but you can only fool the brain so much that fantasy is real.

If we had the eyes to see the spiritual world, we would no longer see opaque bodies and elements, separated by empty space. Everything would be divine light commanded to form this thing or that thing, and to allow it to do this or to do that. We would see rivers of light flowing through everything and up and down from Heaven, a completely spiritual reality.

None of this light would be the least bit physical. It would be comprised of holy sparks, *Nitzotzei Kedushah*, small but powerful "packages" of divine light and will. They are the spiritual atoms of Creation, if you will, made up in divine names. They are the life force of Creation, without which nothing can exist let alone function in any meaningful way.

If you moved your arm, you would see the sparks move. The energy expended to make the movement would free sparks that would then ascend upward. The greater the energy required, including the will involved in the movement, the more sparks used and freed. The greater the holiness of the act, the more readily the sparks can ascend.

Because evil takes sparks as well. There is only one source of life in Creation, and that is God. His sparks are the way He grants and supports it. It is our allowance, decided by God on *Rosh Hashanah*. How we spend it is our choice for which we are held accountable, if not at the moment then later on.

If we use our sparks to learn Torah and perform mitzvos, we elevate sparks, rectify the world, and build our portion in the World-to-Come. If a person sins, they profane the sparks, strengthen the reality of impurity, and become punishable as a means to rectify the sparks they damaged...if they don't do *teshuvah*—repent—in time.

It is a multi-step process. First the sparks have to be elevated out of the *Klipos*,[5] after which they enter the *sefirah* of *Malchus* to be cleansed and prepared for their as-

---

[5] The spiritual basis of all impurity and evil in Creation.

cent to higher levels in the *sefiros*.[6] It is this ascent that will build them into individual *partzufim*, just as gestation allows the embryo to become a fetus.

The *Malchus* is female. *Zehr Anpin* is the male. It is the ascension of the sparks from *Malchus* through the *sefiros* of *Zehr Anpin* (*Yesod* to *Hod* to *Netzach*, etc.) that triggers a *zivug* between him and *Malchus*, and the addition of light to allow the sparks to grow in intensity and ascend even further, to the level of *Binah*.

The main *zivug* in the *sefiros* is between *Chochmah* and *Binah*, otherwise known as *Abba*—Father—and *Imma*—Mother. The light created on this level is far more intense than that created on lower levels, another way of saying that the lower level of light is more filtered. It is the sparks that ascend from *Zehr Anpin* to *Binah* that trigger this level of *zivug*.

But being so high up in the system, it takes a lot more spiritual oomph to get the sparks to this level. For example, praying sends sparks up, but it is the intention behind them that determine how high. Learning Torah elevates sparks, but it is the level of Torah and the sacrifice to learn it that determines how high the sparks will reach. Without

---

[6] It's like dropping a huge amount of gold pieces into a massive swamp, and then having to recover them. That's what God did with the holy sparks prior to Creation, in order to give man the opportunity to recover them from the "swamp" and play a role in the perfection of Creation. The cleaning off the sparks begins to occur once the sparks reach to the level of *Malchus*.

the proper spiritual energy, they can fall very short and have little impact.

Why should it be any different when it comes to God than it is when it comes to people? It is the heartfelt plea that moves people to help because it sounds sincere and shows gratitude for the assistance. A perfunctory request is usually met with a perfunctory response.

This is what it says:

The sacrifices of God are a broken spirit. O God, You will not despise a broken and crushed heart. (Tehillim 51:19)

In life, it is the broken spirit that cries out to God. It is the crushed heart that yearns for help. When people know this and put themselves into their service of God, then He blesses them with light and success. When we forget this and serve Him robotically, then He can cause a broken spirit or crushed heart to kickstart their system.

Again, none of this is for God Himself. It is all for us. We are the beneficiaries of our own self-sacrifice and sincerity. It breeds humility and self-honesty. It builds us, and more importantly, it empowers us. It gives us the opportunity to make a difference because our prayers and Torah learning and just plain good deeds can ascend and trigger all kinds of fantastic things in the *sefiros*.

Now look at the world. There is so little real God awareness and interest. Comparisons are being made between the people in modernized countries and those who lived in *Sdom* just prior to its complete destruction. Falsehood is rampant as is sexual promiscuity. Evil gets away with murder, *literally*.

The Jewish people are struggling as well. A minority keep Torah on some level, and there is a lack of unity even amongst the most devoted. Communities that were once strongholds, places that elevated sparks better than anyone else, are also being impacted negatively. The patient does not look well.

And just as the outside of a person reflects what is going on inside the person, the "look" of the world reveals what is happening on the level of the sparks. That is the level, as we saw regarding the Ten Martyrs, that determines the direction of history.

At the end of the day, the needs of Creation are far more important than the whims of people, which is why the world has already suffered countless wars and tragedies. History is more about getting all of the sparks out of the *Klipos* and back to their holy sources than it is about the people doing it, especially when their focus is really just personal gain.

If you understand the system, then you can know what to do with your life. You can appreciate the opportunity of a single act, even if you can't see it do its thing… even if the results fail to reveal what has occurred on the spiritual plane. You understand the importance of self-sacrifice and a sincere heart when serving God on any level.

If you understand the system, then you can look at the world and see how the system that runs it has been compromised. There are just not enough sparks being elevated out of the *Klipos* to keep the system running to capacity. On the contrary, it almost seems as if Creation is folding in on itself...like it did in Rebi Akiva's time, or more recently, in the period leading up to the Holocaust.

This is what the Torah warned us about in *Parashas Bechukosai* and then later again in *Parashas Ki Savo*. It sounds from there as if the consequence of a sin is angering God, the consequence of which is divine punishment. The real consequence is that an insufficient amount of sparks are elevated which weakens the system, and that brings its own punishment.

It's like a doctor warning their patient to eat better or risk becoming ill. If the patient listens, then they will enjoy good health. If they don't, their body will begin to break down on its own and their health will fail. The doctor doesn't even have to know about the decision because the body has been built to do this on its own.

Likewise, God doesn't have to even get angry enough to punish the world. The fuel of Creation and history is *Nitzotzei Kedushah*. If we "feed" them to the system, then Creation remains healthy and prosperous. If we don't it begins to wither and die, like any other being in Creation.

The thing is, God may let a flower, or even a living being do that. The loss might be difficult for some, but it won't stop Creation in its tracks. God will not, however, let that happen to Creation, which is why He intervenes directly in history when the system is in danger of shutting down.

Historically, that has rarely been good news for man.

Fighting *Gevurah*

We spoke about *Gevurah* as *sefirah*. But history has been about *Gevurah* as a force that affects all aspects of our lives. It has been the source of tremendous good, and it has been the source of tremendous evil. Anyone who is waiting for *Moshiach* to come is really waiting for the remaining *Gevuros* to be rectified. The latter is the reason for the former.

Both Yitzchak *Avinu* and Eisav *HaRasha* are examples of the two extremes of *Gevurah*. Yitzchak used the force of *Gevurah* to work on himself to the point of spiritual perfection, even eliminating his *yetzer hara*. Eisav used *Gevurah* to impose his will on others and become the complete opposite of his father.

There are many things in life that work the same way. Water quenches thirst and saves from death. But water can also become a tsunami and wipe out an entire coastal town. Light illuminates darkness, but it can also blind a person and leave them in darkness for the rest of their life.

Likewise, *Gevurah* is *tzimtzum*. It constricts. When someone gets angry, it is the result of *Gevurah*. If they are strict, it is because of *Gevurah*. If they are evil, they have become an embodiment of *Gevurah*. It takes *Gevurah* to destroy them. War is pure *gevurah*.

But self-disciple is also a function of *Gevurah*. So is loyalty. It takes a lot of *Gevurah* to make meaningful and necessary sacrifices in life. *Chesed*-based people are loved, but heroes are the result of channeled *Gevurah,* and admired because of their mastery of *Gevurah*. For a lot of people, doing *chesed* is an act of *Gevurah*.

There are many ways to describe the purpose of life, but on a *kabbalistic* level, it is called *Mituk HaGevuros*— Sweetening of the *Gevuros*. Every time a *gevurah* is used to further the purpose of Creation, the *gevurah* is said to have been sweetened, or rectified, and Creation is one more *gevurah* closer to its goal of perfection. When the last *gevurah* is sweetened, *Moshiach* will come, evil will end, and life will be ideal.[1]

Mituk can happen because of us, or through us. Using *Gevurah* in a Torah manner is rectification *because* of

---

[1] *Drushei Olam HaTohu, Chelek 2, Drush 4, Anaf 17.*

man. Using *Gevurah* in non-Torah ways causes rectification *through* man, especially when the *gevurah* boomerangs and becomes the source of the person's punishment.[2] The suffering that results has a cleansing effect on the misused *gevuros*, after which they can join those already rectified.

This is the deeper meaning of this:

> *See, I have placed before you today the life and the good, and the death and the evil…choose life that you will live… (Devarim 30:15, 19)*

It tells us to choose to sweeten the *Gevuros* through life, that is, through the performance of *mitzvos* and the learning of Torah. It tells us to not allow situations to arise where the *Gevuros* have to be used up through us, like during the Holocaust. All the horrible and unimaginable suffering was a massive *mituk* of *Gevuros* on a national scale. It did not show that the generation was more evil than others. It showed how far behind the world was in *Mituk HaGevuros*.

The Torah is not saying that anyone in their right mind would deliberately choose death. The Torah is warning that when we don't choose to do that which rectifies the *Gevuros* in Creation, it is tantamount to choosing death. Eventually they'll result in war and destruction, and in many instances in increased anti-Semitism and pogroms.

---

[2] *Drushei Olam HaTohu, Chelek 2, Drush 4, Anaf 17.*

The issue is time. There may be two times for *Moshiach* to come, but there is a also a *final* time. History has an expiry date, and the rectification of all the *Gevuros* must be by that time. If it didn't, then perhaps history could continue for thousands of more years, and be a lot safer. But history does, and it has to compensate for where man falls short in meeting history's deadline.

It also says that the *Gevuros* know this. They know somehow that their time to run amok is limited, and they will fight to the death when that time approaches. That's when history will really look wild, and people will really live unbridled. They'll think that they're just taking advantage of the moment to have a good time, but the truth is that they will just be vehicles for the *Gevuros* to lash out one last time.

Violence will increase. Wars will start up. The world will seem out of control. It may be made to appear like politics of the day, but that is just the means for the *Gevuros* to do their thing, not the cause. They are the cause, and the enemy, until they can be sweetened and converted to the side of good, kind of like doing outreach on Eisav to make him like Yitzchak.

In fact, that is what Yitzchak tried to do to his son. He knew who Eisav was and how he lived. But he also knew that Eisav had the potential to be a Dovid *HaMelech*, who for all-intents-and-purposes, was Eisav converted to the side of God.

This is what the blessing would have done to Eisav

had he received it.[3] It would have rectified his *Gevuros* and used them for the service of God, as Dovid *HaMelech* did later on in history, partly through deed and partly through all the personal suffering he had to endure. And this is why he didn't reject God because of it, because he knew and trusted the system:

> *O Lord, my God, if I have done this, if there is any injustice in my hands; if I repaid the one who did evil to me, and I stripped my adversary into emptiness, may the enemy pursue my soul and overtake [me] and trample my life to the ground, and cause my soul to rest in the dust forever.* (Tehillim 7:4-6)

That is how you build a *melech*, and *Malchus*. The *Malchus* in essence is *Gevuros*, being the farthest of the 10 *sefiros* from the Source of light. When all of its *Gevuros* are rectified after thousands of years of history, the *Malchus* will finally be fitting to be God's kingdom on earth. All doubt that anyone ever had about God will vanish like smoke since they were only the result of unrectified *Gevuros* in the first place.

Negative prophecies don't have to come true, but

---

[3] *Parashas Toldos.* First Yitzchak sent Eisav on a hunting mission to bring back food for him for the purpose of starting the process of *mituk*. That too would have worked had God not decided against it for reasons unknown at the time to Yitzchak.

often do. The Talmud's predictions for the End-of-Days[4] are more than gloomy, they are frightening. They basically describe the world the way it has become today: rampant falsehood, heretical governments, promiscuity, etc. In short, the *Gevuros* making their last stand.

Do they know that they bring redemption quicker by increasing their evil? Perhaps. But they're probably so overjoyed at the destruction they are causing that they put that issue on the back burner in the meantime. Or perhaps they don't and will only find out after they have taken their toll on mankind in the final moments of history.

It is not conventional warfare. We can battle against the representatives of the *Gevuros*, all those people and things that do their bidding as if it is their own, but that is not proving to be the successful approach. On the contrary, it just seems to make them stronger in the end.

Attack their fuel line. Every war needs fuel to run all its vehicles and machinery, which is why armies have constantly tried to bomb enemy fuel lines. This was a major issue for the Germans prior to the end of World War II, especially in North Africa. Their lack of fuel helped to end the war quicker, and in favor of the allies.

It's not different when it comes to fighting a spiritual war. The only difference is the kind of fuel used, and how the supply of it to the enemy can be stopped. In the case of the *Klipos*, the fuel is *Nitzotzei Kedushah*, and stopping the

---

[4] *Sotah* 49b; *Sanhedrin* 97a.

flow of it means using up as many sparks as possible for the right things.

That's one of the advantages of a spiritual war. In a physical war, you have to physically get to the enemy's supply lines. In a spiritual war, you can get to *Nitzotzei Kedushah* from anywhere. You can do *mitzvos* or learn Torah on the other side of the world, even on the other side of the universe, and still draw Holy Sparks away from the *Klipos* and weaken the *Gevuros*.

The better the *mitzvah* is performed, a function of attention to detail and sincerity, the more sparks are drawn away from the *Klipos*. Thus it says:

> *And now, O Israel, what does God, your God, ask of you? Only to fear God, your God, to walk in all His ways and to love Him, and to worship God, your God, with all your heart and with all your soul, to keep the commandments of God and His statutes, which I command you this day, for your good. (Devarim 10:12-13)*

Obedience is not the goal. It is the means. The goal of life and history is to round up all the relevant sparks and leave the *Klipos* empty of every last one. When that happens, *Moshiach* comes, the world is righted forever,[5] and history can move on to bigger and better things like pre-

---

[5] *Sha'ar HaGilgulim*, Introduction 20.

paring for eternal life in the World-to-Come.

That is a function of teamwork, the more the better. And every team is only as good as the efforts of its team members towards the goal. Rarely does any team accomplish its goal without a concerted effort by all those on the team. And that means...

Through Teshuvah

eshuvah is central to a Torah way of life and getting to the World-to-Come. Though we may not deserve a second chance, but God *miraculously* gives us one anyhow, and a third, and fourth, etc. As long as a person wakes up in time to the gravity of their error, they can right their wrong by regretting it, confessing to their sin, and then trying hard not to repeat it.[1]

A gift?

Unquestionably.

A weapon against *Gevurah* and the *Klipos*?

One of the best.

---

[1] *Yad Chazakah, Hilchos Teshuvah.*

To begin with, *Kabbalah* teaches, the Hebrew word *teshuvah*, spelled *Tav-Shin-Vav-Bais-Heh*, is really the word *teshuv*, *Tav-Shin-Vav-Bais*, and the letter *Heh*. It means, "return *Heh*." When a person does *teshuvah*, they return the *Heh*.

Which *Heh*? The final *Heh* of God's four-letter name that we do not pronounce the way it is written. Instead, we refer to it as the *Shem Hovayah*, because the name *Hovayah* is the same four letters just rearranged in a way that can be said the way it is written.

Why does the *Heh* of God's ineffable name need to be returned, and where did it go in the first place?

It has to do with the impact of a sin on the *sefiros*, specifically the *Malchus*. To begin with, the four letters of God's name actually correspond to the 10 *sefiros*. The *Yud* corresponds to *Chochmah*, and the crown on the *Yud* to *Keser*. The first *Heh* corresponds to *Binah*, the *Vav* corresponds to the six *sefiros* of *Chesed* through *Yesod*, and the final *Heh*, to *Malchus*.

Sin causes a separation of the final *Heh* from the upper three letters. This translates into our world becoming less spiritual and more heretical. As the *Heh* becomes distanced from the *Yesod*, less divine light is able to flow to the *Malchus*...and us. This is the technical dynamic that results in what we call *hester panim*, the *hiding of God's face*, described here:

I will become very angry at them on that day, and I

will abandon them and hide My face from them. They will be devoured, and plagued by many evils that will distress them, and will say, "Do we not suffer because God has left us?" (Devarim 31:17)

Teshuvah therefore has the reverse effect. It has the power to draw the *Heh* back towards the *Yesod* and, hence, *teshuv Heh*. It may seem like all a person has done is shown regret and said sorry for the sin. It's not as if the world dramatically changes and a bunch of atheists and agnostics do their own *teshuvah* because of it.

Well, at least as far as *we* can see. Who knows the level of impact a person's *teshuvah* has on them and the world? Perhaps much greater than God lets us see at this time, because if we could see it so clearly, many might be driven to do *teshuvah* for this reason, and not out of personal regret.

On the other hand, the *Gemora* says that, when it is necessary God will "inspire" *teshuvah* from the outside:

Rebi Eliezer said, "If Israel will repent then they will be redeemed, and if they will not, then they will not [be redeemed]."

Rebi Yehoshua said to him, "If they do not repent they will not be redeemed?! Rather, The Holy One, Blessed is He, will raise up a king who will make decrees as difficult as Haman's, and Israel will repent and return to the right path." (*Sanhedrin* 97b)

On the surface of it, it would seem that *teshuvah* will be necessary to merit redemption. But the Gemora says elsewhere that it can happen whether the generation merits it or not,[2] and the Vilna *Gaon* said that it will certainly happen the latter way. So why impose *teshuvah* on the nation through evil leaders?

Because technically, redemption *is* the return of the *Heh* to the three upper letters. It has to happen because redemption cannot happen without it. The only question is *how* it will happen, a choice that has been left to us, the Jewish people. Either we realize the need for *teshuvah* on our own or be forced to realize it by the events of the day. In Mordechai's time, it almost resulted in a Holocaust. In the 1940s, it did.

Because even though there are still those who cling to the idea that the return of the Jewish homeland to the Jewish people in 1948 had nothing to do with redemption, history and *hashkofah* say otherwise. The Holocaust says otherwise.

To begin with, the events of 1948 were only a technical formality. The real reality is that each time a Jew made *aliyah* over the hundreds of years since the *GR"A's* time[3] and settled the land in some way, *Eretz Yisroel* became more the Jewish people's possession. He began the process of *Kibbutz Golios* in his time because he believed

---

[2] *Sanhedrin* 97a.
[3] He lived from 1720–1790.

the final redemption was at hand, and that was true regardless of how it happened.[4]

And the official world acceptance of a modern Jewish homeland didn't just happen in 1948, or 5708 from Creation, because the war just happened to end in 1945, and it just happened to take three years to declare the state and be accepted by the UN. Just the other way around. Official declaration of the Jewish homeland *had* to occur, for historic reasons going back to Creation, in 1948.

Therefore the war ended in 1945, which meant it had to begin in 1939, after Kristallnacht in 1938, etc. It's the *keitzin,* the divinely set end times that lead to some aspect of redemption, that set the tone for history. And if we don't take notice of them, then they will cause events to happen that will catch our attention, as they did in the 1930s and so many other times in history before an upcoming *keitz.*

Some may argue, "How much *teshuvah* resulted from the Holocaust? On the contrary, so many religious Jews were either murdered or survived and turned their backs on God! If anything, there was reason not to give *Eretz Yisroel* to the Jewish people..."

The answer to the question is a warning to the future. When a person does *teshuvah* on their own, it's not only

---

[4] See my book, *Drowning In Pshat* for a detailed explanation, according to *Kabbalah* and historic sources, of how God often brings redemption in convoluted ways if a *keitz* comes and the Jewish people aren't "ready" for it.

on their own terms, but it ends happily. A person comes closer to God and feels better about themself. They may even enjoy some extra help from Heaven at what they do, and influence others to act similarly, increasing their merit now and later.

When we don't do *teshuvah* on our own, it is obviously a different story. It will change us, but not necessarily in a way that will make us feel better about life or ourself. A person might even feel more distant from God in the end, because that is often the result of suffering that we did not go looking for. It saddens people, depresses people, even makes them resentful.

But the suffering is the suffering. It humbles a person's spirit. It may not be self-sacrifice, but it is certainly sacrifice. Suffering forces a person to give some of their life, and whether they choose to do it or is imposed upon them, it still uses up sparks, tempers *Gevuros*, and advances the cause of redemption. How much more so on a national scale, and to the extent that it happened between 1942 and 1945.

People who survived the Holocaust but who gave up their belief in God were called by the *Gedolim* after the war, "Holy Disbelievers." Not everyone could witness what they witnessed, experience what they experienced, and come out with their faith intact. But by witnessing what they witnessed and experiencing what they experienced, they became holy to God in any case, and even more so those whose faith in God survived with them.

It's like a son who asks his father for some money to buy something. If the father happily gives the money, both the son and father get pleasure from the purchase. If the father gives the money begrudgingly, neither fully enjoys what the son buys, but that doesn't stop the purchase from going through. Likewise, suffering fixes the world, even if only temporarily.

Thus, when people say things like, "*Eretz Yisroel* was built on the ashes of the Holocaust," it is not figurative. Getting the land "back" at that time required the *Heh* of God's Name to come closer to the upper three letters. The Torah learned and the *mitzvos* performed at that time were clearly not enough. There was not enough *teshuvah* occurring at the time to do it. But the addition of the suffering of all the Jews at that time was…

It's not even clear how many people did full *teshuvah* in Mordechai's time. *Megillas Esther* ends off on a kind of a sour note by saying that Mordechai was only respected by a majority of the Jews of his time. The *Ibn Ezra* says that jealousy had a lot to do with that.

The *Zohar* says[5] there was a chance to bring the final redemption at that time but wasn't used. The upper wellsprings of light and wisdom had opened at that time to facilitate it, but when so many chose to remain in Bavel they closed again, not to open again until the End-of-Days. Here we are today, thousands of years and three exiles later, still

---

[5] *Zohar, Shemos* 9b.

waiting for that to happen.

It turns out that their three days of fasting with the torment they suffered under Haman was enough to free them from their situation. It bought them redemption from Haman, but not redemption from history. That was a taller order and cost more. . .requiring them to sacrifice the comfort of Bavel for the godliness of *Eretz Yisroel*. Unpaid, history and exile continued for thousands of years more.

This is a mistake that we make too often. The fact that exile can be so pleasant does not mean God approves of it. It's like taking care of your health only once it starts to fail, which often is too late. The point is to use good health to maintain good health, to use the quiet and pleasant times of exile to work out redemption.

In other words, don't wait for God to get angry before doing *teshuvah*. First of all, it may be too little too late. And secondly, it is *teshuvah* from fear, and not *teshuvah* from love. The first doesn't have the same rectifying power as the second because it doesn't mean that the "sinner" has completely changed their view. It just means they're smart enough to avoid the negative consequence of repeating the sin.

The *gematria* of *ahava*—love is equal to the *gematria* of *echad*—one, because that is what love does, it unifies. And when a person unifies with God, they unify the *Heh* with the rest of the letters. This is the *real* and lasting *tikun*.

This is why, as the *Gemora* says, *teshuvah* from fear

does not turn past sins into merits as does *teshuvah* from love.[6] By rejoining the *Heh* to the upper three letters, the world is spiritually cleansed, especially the sparks that were used for the sin. Since it was the person's *teshuvah* that did this, it is to their credit.

But *teshuvah* from fear does not completely return the *Heh*, so the sullied sparks only have a partial cleansing, if at all. Other things may have to happen in the world to make that happen, and though the person themself may be off the hook for their sin, they don't get the merit of freeing the sparks from the grasp of the *Klipos*. And we *need* those sparks to enlarge our portion in the World-to-Come.[7]

---

[6] *Yoma* 86b.

[7] A person's portion in the World-to-Come is constructed from all the sparks they managed to free from the *Klipos* and cause to ascend their proper place in the *sefiros*.

Through *Tefillah*

hat's really going on when a person prays? How does that impact the sparks? It all depends on how you pray. If you just go through the motions of prayer, not that much. If you really put yourself into your *dovening*, then *a lot*.

It helps to know what is actually going on when you *doven* or make a *brochah*. Is prayer just another thing we have been commanded to do, which we dutifully carry out, some better than others? Is it simply about asking God for what we want and thanking Him for what we get? Or is it a specific process we engage in to enable us to impact our daily situation by how we do it?

The *Nefesh HaChaim*, in *Sha'ar* 2, discusses prayer in

detail and how it "feeds" the *sefiros*. *Shacharis, Mincha,* and *Ma'ariv* are just different "feeding" times throughout the day. And what do *sefiros* consume if not divine light, *Ohr Ain Sof,* drawn down by our *tefillos.*

The main idea that the *Nefesh HaChaim*[1] deals with has to do with the word *boruch,* with which we start most blessings. How does one bless God when He is already perfect and cannot be improved upon, as the word blessing implies? He not only *has* everything, He *is* everything, so there is nothing that could be added to His existence.

He answers that though we cannot add to or take anything away from God's existence, He has made His revelation flexible. It can be increased or decreased, depending upon the actions of people and the needs of history. When we say, *"Blessed are You, God…"* we are really saying, "may this blessing increase Your light and awareness of Your existence in the world."

It won't, however, if you don't believe it yourself. If a person prays without sincerity, then what are they saying about the reality of God in life? If they act as if prayer is unimportant, how can their *tefillos* accomplish the opposite? Instead, they deny the *sefiros* their due and really, themselves their blessing. Our blessing is just the light that we draw through the *sefiros.*

But it should be clearer by now that any light that comes down must first begin with light going up. Sparks

---

[1] Rabbi Chaim Volozhin (1749–1821).

have to be elevated out of the *Klipos*, sent upwards to cause *zivugim*—pairing in the *sefiros*—before light can be added and returned to us as blessing and success. And each blessing has been carefully crafted, by prophets and *kabbalists*,[2] to do exactly this in its own specific way.

For example, the *brochah* in *Shemonah Esrai* right before *Kedushah* is, "Blessed are You, God, Who resurrects the dead." This is one of the 13 Principles of Faith, that at some time in the future, God will resurrect the dead well into the Messianic Era in preparation for the next stages of history. The question is, why is the *brochah* in Present Tense, and not Future Tense?

It's not a question that has bothered the millions of people who have said this blessing millions of times since the *Anshei Knesses HaGedolah* established it.[3] And there really is no answer for it on the level of *Pshat*, the most obvious level of Torah learning, other than, *"The Anshei Knesses HaGedolah* had their reasons."

They did, and it is *kabbalistic* because it has to do with what happened *prior* to Creation, and that is completely *kabbalistic*, something called *Sheviras HaKeilim— the breaking of the vessels,* and also *Missas HaMelachim, the death of the kings.*

Part of the process of making Creation was pre-world

------

[2] *Anshei Knesses HaGedolah*, the Men of the Great Assembly. See https://www.jewishhistory.org/the-men-of-the-great-assembly/.

[3] See the previous note.

worlds. There's never been another world like ours, and there never will be. There doesn't have to be. God knew exactly what He wanted when He started, and exactly how to get there. Part of "getting there" were some early stages of creation, one of the earliest being *Sheviras HaKeilim*.

We know what happened and why, but that is too complicated to go into right now. The point is that God wanted a world that could support human free will, and that necessitated the creation of some kind of evil so that man could be tempted to go after it. This way doing the right thing could be a challenge and something worth rewarding in the World-to-Come.

The result was a perfectly imperfect world. The imperfect part is obvious. The perfect part is because it is exactly what God wanted and it gives man the opportunity to transform it into a perfectly perfect world. A billion things may go on in life around the world each day, but the point of all of it is the eradication of evil and the perfection of Creation.

A perfectly imperfect world is no big deal for a human. We *are* imperfect and have a more difficult time doing things perfectly. But God *is* perfection, and everything exists inside of Him. So how can something imperfect even exist at all?

It is a philosophical question up for philosophical debate, but the means is not. God created *sefiros* whose intended incompletion left them incapable of a sustained existence. As a result, at a certain time in the process in a certain way, each of the seven lowest pre-Creation *sefiros* broke, or died, as planned. The main lights they once contained ascended to their sources above, while a fragment of their light fell below as *nitzotzei kedushah*—Holy Sparks— with a seemingly infinite amount of fragments that were once the *keilim*—vessels—that contained the light.

This resulted in the creation of the *Klipos*, the more *chitzoni*—external and waste-like elements of the vessels, and the next stage of Creation called *Tohu*—Null, the primordial chaos. The Torah mentions *Tohu* after Creation, but as the *Zohar* explains, it actually preceded Creation.[4]

Creation itself as we know it was the process of extracting out the necessary broken pieces and sparks in order to re-build them into the *sefiros* we now have and which are the basis of our Creation. Because they came from the *shivrei keilim*—broken vessels, they had an inherent spiritual imperfection built into them that could allow the *Klipos* to continue, for evil to continue, and for man to have free will.

When Adam *HaRishon* sinned, he not only did not finish off the work God started, but he even reversed much of it. Broken pieces and sparks returned to the *Klipos* and *Tohu*, to be rectified once again over the course of history. Every time God creates something, it uses broken pieces and sparks. By making the broken pieces and sparks part of Creation again, God has resurrected them, given them new

---

4 *Zohar, Bereishis* 16a.

life.

We acknowledge this in the *brochah* of resurrection of the dead, a process that has been ongoing since Creation itself. We are thanking God for the world we live in, which is completely a function of constantly reviving *shivrei keilim and nitzotzei kedushah.* When enough has been done, then the Messianic Era will begin, and the world will become increasingly perfect.

HaEl HaKadosh

And holy too, because it is the same thing. The more perfect the world, the holier it becomes. The *Kohen Gadol* wore the words, *Kodesh L'Hashem*—Holy to God—because that is the purpose of life, to make the world holy. Every time holy sparks are drawn out of the *Klipos* through Torah and *mitzvos*, the world becomes holier.

Da'as

But you need *da'as* to do this. In fact, you need *dayah*, *binah*, and *haskel*. You need to know about the idea, you need to understand the idea, and then you need to be wise enough to find the opportunities to make it happen.

It is amazing how many smart people there are in the world, and yet so few people know what life is about and how to make the most of it. As smart as they are, they are not smart enough to figure out that they have a *yetzer hara* that prevents them from using their opportunity of life in the most meaningful way possible.

On the contrary, some of the most brilliant minds have used their intelligence in only secular ways. Yes, they have accomplished a tremendous amount, but no, not in the most spiritually beneficial way possible. They have advanced mankind scientifically and technologically, and that may have some spiritual benefits as well, but not to the extent that someone does when they make the world a *holier* place. They use up sparks, but not that many.

In fact, some of the most important acts a person can ever do for Creation may have no obvious effects. When it comes to the secular world, seeing is believing. If a sick person takes a medicine and gets better shortly after, it is easy to believe that the medicine healed them. But if a sick person prayed, or had someone else pray for them, and they got better, a non-believer will assume it was just a coincidence.

The *Gemora* says that *tzedakah* saves a person from death and brings examples of when it did.[5] But if it happens today, many will have a difficult time believing that the act of charity actually did the work, especially since some very charitable people have died or become very sick anyhow.

There are tests you can perform to confirm the positive or negative effect of a medicine. But how do you do the same thing with a spiritual medicine? Without a

---

[5] *Shabbos* 156a.

prophet to confirm the connection between the recovery and the spiritual act, you can only have faith that it is there. And even many "religious" people today don't have *that* much faith in spiritual cures.

That is the difference between *dayah*, *binah*, and *haskel*. *Dayah* and *binah* are necessary to reach the level of *da'as*, but *haskel* is *da'as* itself.[6] You don't only *know* something is true, you can *feel* its truth. It's not an emotion, but a state of mind, a level of awareness, and ultimately, a gift from God.

Teshuvah and Forgiveness

There are two parts to the *teshuvah* process, *teshuvah* from our side and *kaparah*—atonement—from God's side. We seek atonement through *teshuvah*, but only God can grant it. He decides when a person has done proper *teshuvah* worthy of *teshuv-Heh*, the return of the *Heh* to the rest of the letters of God's name.

The prophet once cried out to God about the heartless sacrifices brought by the Jewish people of his time. They were *halachically* correct, but lacked sincerity. The people had just been going through the motions somehow thinking that it would be enough to keep God from getting angry at them.

But the proof was in the sparks. You can fool some of

---

[6] In *Nusach Sephard* it is *Chochmah*, *Binah*, and *Da'as*, corresponding to the *sefiros* themselves.

the people some of the time, but you can't fool the sparks any of the time. The sparks did not ascend, and history fell behind schedule, necessitating drastic action from God's side. The inevitable result became destruction of the Temple and exile to Babylonia.

Redemption

This *brochah* is a gear shift. Until now, the emphasis was on what an individual needs to do to act on of behalf of God in the process of world perfection. Now the focus becomes national, what the collection body of *Klal Yisroel* requires to be the instrument of world *tikun* we were taken out of Egypt to be.

As mentioned earlier, the *Shechinah* works through the Jewish people when the Jewish people work on behalf of the *Shechinah,* which becomes more difficult when we are in exile. During a hostile exile it is because of oppression, but during a friendly exile it is because of assimilation and intermarriage. Either way there is a slowdown of spark elevation, and increased sin can give sparks over to the *Klipos*.

There is another important point to keep in mind. Redemption is a lot like transferring money from an account in one country to another account in a different country. The transfer is only complete when the entire amount has been transferred.

Likewise, redemption is about transferring a certain amount of sparks from one location to another, the ultimate location being *Eretz Yisroel*. It is only "complete" when the last of the divinely specified sparks have been "transferred" to the next intended location.

That can happen one of two ways. Either a person physically moves to that location, taking the spark within them. Or, as we saw in the Plague of Darkness in Egypt, and countless other times after that, Jews are killed in their current location, thereby freeing up their sparks to move on to their next location. That seems to be the choice that we are supposed to make.

To make that choice possible, we have to maintain a *geulah* consciousness. We have to think about redemption all the time and, most important of all, we have to *want* redemption. So *Chazal* put a reminder of this right at the beginning of *Shemonah Esrai*.

But this *brochah* is also in *Present Tense*. We don't bless God as the God Who will *eventually* redeem us again, and hopefully for good, but as the God Who redeems Israel now, in the Present, and for two good reasons.

First of all, "Israel" is also a euphemism for the holy sparks that God is constantly redeeming by taking them out of the *Klipos* and transferring them to the side of holiness. Secondly, *geulah* is an ongoing process, and it can take place on the level of the individual as well as the national level.

When God arranged it that the UN vote in favor of the acceptance of a Jewish homeland back in 1948, it was obvious to many that God was in the process of redeeming the Jewish people. But when God had President Roosevelt drop his running mate of three elections for Harry S. Truman in the 1947 election, no one knew at the time that he would be a catalyst for a favorable UN vote.

So many things necessary for a redemption in any time period occur out of eyeshot, either because we can't see them happening or because at the time, they seemed to be working in the opposite direction of *geulah*, like Haman's rise to power. We might not be consciously and constantly involved in the *geulah* process, but God is.

Health

Health has everything to do with holy sparks. The health of the body depends upon its attachment to the soul, which increases or decreases depending upon the amount of holy sparks a person "consumes," either directly from food or supernaturally, as was the case with Moshe *Rabbeinu* who did not eat or drink for 40 days and 40 nights on *Har Sinai*.

The medical profession speaks about nutrients, which were discovered over time based upon trial and error and a better understanding of the make up of food and of the human body. But nutrients are only healthy because of the amount of sparks they possess, and their health benefit is just the physical manifestation of this spiritual reality.

But at the end of the day, it all comes down to God,

life and death and health and illness. There are people who live very unspiritual lives who live healthily ever after, and people who take care of themselves who die suddenly and at a young age. It's God decision and His alone.

Sometimes it is just a matter of maintaining a certain perception to make free will possible. Everyone would run after the sparks if it was clear that they are what keep us going. God wants us to run after holy sparks because it is the right thing to do, and our means of implementing His will.

Sometimes it has to do with personal *tikun* that can be left over from previous incarnations. In other words, all things being equal, how we are living should keep us healthy. But, the need for personal *tikun* requires *yesurim*, some kind of suffering related to some health issue.

So, we do the best we can to intake as many *nitzotzei kedushah* as we can but pray to God it is reason enough to grant us good health, to let the sparks do their thing. Illness uses up a lot of sparks, but it is also debilitating and interferes with consciously and actively being part of the program of world rectification.

Parnassah

Though we talk about earning a *parnassah*, about making a living, we actually don't. The *Gemora* says[7] and

---

[7] *Brochos* 17a.

the *Leshem* concurs,[8] that everything a Jew earns, no matter how much and how easily, is really more like a stipend from God to allow us to do the work He made us to do.

The centrality of currency is just stark testimony to the fact that life costs. Though we constantly look for free things, the bare fact is that they do not exist because it is not the way the world was made. On the contrary, the "free" things in life may cost us the most of all, denying us the opportunity to elevate sparks out of the *Klipos* through will and self-sacrifice.

Getting paid and paying for things is one of the main ways the sparks get transferred from place to place. When it allows someone to accomplish something meaningful, the sparks within it are released and elevated furthering the cause of *tikun* and redemption. When "money" is used wastefully, the sparks go to the *Klipos*.

When we ask God to grant us *parnassah*, we are really asking Him to grant us a significant portion of *nitzotzei kedushah* to elevate. We are asking Him for the opportunity to be a contributor to world rectification, and increased reward in the World-to-Come.

If anything, we are not asking God for increased comfort and enough money to retire one day. We are asking for an ongoing flow of divine light that we can use to accomplish great spiritual things as partners of God in the fulfillment of the master plan for Creation.

---

[8] *Hakdamos uSha'arim, Sha'ar* 6, *Perek* 9.

Ingathering

This *brochah* is about *Kibbutz Golios*, the ingathering of the Jewish people from wherever they have settled in the Diaspora, back to *Eretz Yisroel*. And as mentioned earlier, the ingathering is of sparks, either inside people themselves, or just as the sparks themselves.

The *Gemora* mentions that the Jewish people go into exile to make converts,[9] which is hard to understand considering we tend not to proselytize and even discourage potential converts. And how many gentiles actually end up converting to Judaism while we are in their lands?

The *Leshem* explains that "converts" includes more than people.[10] There are countless sparks in the Diaspora that need to be "converted" as well from the side of impurity to the side of holiness. Just eating in the Diaspora or getting paid a salary does this. It comes from a gentile source, is used for a *mitzvah*, and after that ascends to its source in *kedushah*. Hence, this *brochah* is also in Present Tense because the process has been ongoing since Creation.

Return of Judges

The *Gemora* speaks of the importance of judging truthfully in a few places, and the consequences of corruption in the legal system. When judges are honest, then the

---

[9] *Pesachim* 87b.

[10] *Drushei Olam HaTohu, Chelek* 2, *Drush* 4, *Anaf* 12, *Siman* 10; *Sha'ar HaGilgulim*, Introduction 20.

Shechinah joins with them in their judgments.[11] When they are not, the *Shechinah* detests them and their decisions, especially since they force God to right their wrongs.

A corrupt legal decision is the source of despair for the average individual who depends upon it to defend their rights and protect them again injustices. When the legal system fails, then it seems as if there is no one else to turn to, which is very demoralizing since it means that society has fallen.

It also means that the *Chitzonim* have risen in power. Corruption is a function of the *Klipos*, as is depression,[12] and they can only increase their hold on people when they are receiving too many holy sparks. As the *Gemora* warns, this will be the situation right before *Moshiach* comes,[13] and therefore a harbinger of his imminent arrival.

Removal of Slanderers

The slanderers being referred to here are not necessarily irreligious. They can be religious too. But they act in ways that are contrary to the goals of Torah, even though they may think that they are serving the ultimate goals of the Jewish people. They've been wrong, and oftentimes dangerous because they have interfered with the role and safety of the Jewish people.

---

[11] *Brochos* 6a.
[12] *Sha'ar HaGilgulim*, Introduction 38.
[13] *Sotah* 49b.

The *Sitra Achra*, aka *Satan*, aka Angel of Death, is the one pulling on the other end of the tug rope of holy sparks. But unlike a simple tug-of-rope, you can't clearly see the "enemy" or the rope for that matter, and even well-meaning people can find themselves pulling for the wrong side. The *Sitra Achra* takes advantage of people's knowledge gaps and emotional leanings to recruit them to his side without them being the wiser.

But then there are those who are just plain crooked. They live to undermine the Torah world and its objectives. They don't have to be recruited by the *Sitra Achra*. They signed up on their own, and use their positions of influence and power to do their best to interfere with Torah Judaism.

Either way, we need God's help to know who is who, and to overcome whatever it is they throw in our path of world rectification. Ultimately, the *Sitra Achra* works for God, but ever since he first got Adam to eat from the *Aitz HaDa'as Tov v'Ra*, he has excelled at his job to mankind's detriment. It would be a tragic mistake to assume that we can fight him on our own.

The rest of the *Shemonah Esrai*, and all of *tefillah* for that matter, can be understood in the same way. This is especially true of the *brochos* that make direct references to *Moshiach* and *geulah*, like the planting of the "seed" of Dovid, and the return of the *Shechinah* to *Tzion*, both of which are indications of the progress of spark elevation and depend directly on it.

Prayer itself is also an underrated form of spark elevation. Just the act alone requires a quiet form of *mesiras Nefesh*. It's not usually physically strenuous, other than standing up for extended periods of time. But getting your heart and mind into *tefillah* can be more strenuous than more physical *mitzvos* because we have less control over our minds and emotions than we do over our actions.

As a person expends energy to maintain their thinking about God during *tefillah* and what the *brochah* means, sparks are drawn out of the *Klipos* at a rate that depends upon the energy used. That's why the *Klipos* fight back in one way or another, through external or internal distraction. If ever the tug-o-war takes place for sparks with the *Klipos*, it is during *tefillah*.

The people who understand this treat *tefillah* like a soldier might a rapid firing machine gun. The soldier knows that he possesses a very effective and dangerous weapon and treats it accordingly. Likewise, *tefillah* is translated as *arrows* in Aramaic, because they are effective and a deadly weapon against the side of evil that wishes to steal our sparks and use them to their end.

People doven thousands of times throughout the course of their lives. But how many of them have been squandered opportunities to greatly fix themselves and the world?

If Only We Knew

illions of people have walked the earth over the last 5,783 years, but how many have known what is really going on? Seventy-five percent? Fifty-five percent? Twenty-five percent? The number undoubtedly is a lot smaller. A LOT smaller.

How could that be? Did God err in the creation of man? How could He have made a world with so few people who have any idea of what is going on, or what to do? We're talking about God here. Shouldn't we expect a much higher success rate?

It all depends upon how you define success in this case, or more precisely, what God is after. What does *He* expect from history?

If history itself is any indication, it clearly comes down to a very small group of leader types, and the masses. There are the people who rise to the top in one way or another, either for good or for bad, and the large amounts of people who either support or reject them.

It's like a movie set. A movie set may have hundreds of people on it, but the story centers on just two main characters. Likewise, history has its main characters in every generation, and everyone else on the "set" seems to be seconds, part of the background.

Just who is who can depend upon the soul of a person. In *Sha'ar HaGilgulim*, teachings from the *Arizal* about reincarnation and personal growth, it speaks about the different levels of souls. There are always nuances and exceptions to the rule, but for the most part, a person is driven by the soul to become what they do.

This is why some people are frustrated by a lack of accomplishment, and others are happy to simply live from day to day. Some have great aspirations while others have few or none. It is a person's soul that drives them to greatness, or in very many cases, to accept what driven people would call mediocrity.

God never has a complaint about someone who is living up to their potential, be it great or little. The main thing is that a person does what they are here to do, large or small. God is completely just and doesn't play favorites and will judge everyone in a way that will make sense to them as well in the World-to-Come.

This is why when you tell some people how God runs His world, they don't care. They may not even want to know. It just complicates matters for them, and life is complicated enough as it is. Just tell them what they have to do to live a "good" life, and they will do their best to stay with the program.

For some, just the opposite is true. Not only do they want to understand the inner, more *kabbalistic* workings of Creation, they regret not knowing it earlier. If they had known it, they would have done things differently. But, if they had been meant to do things differently, then they would have known it because Divine Providence would have made sure of it.

The question a person has to ask themself is, "Which group do I belong to?" The truth is, if a person is asking this question then chances are they have already answered it. People who are not destined for greatness on some level feel no need to ask such questions, or even think about them. If questions like this matter to you, it is because it matters to your soul, which is trying to get you to look beyond a simple and straightforward life.

This would be the most obvious thing about life if we were only souls. But we're not. We have bodies too, and they are not spiritual at all. Some seem more energetic than others, but each body is instinctual and loves comfort. It's just a question of the kind of comfort a particular body loves.

Laziness, therefore, is not a function of the soul, but

of the body. A soul may not desire to reach the highest of spiritual heights, but it does "instinctually" want to fulfill itself on its own level. But certainly a soul with great spiritual potential is being held back by its host body when the person becomes too lazy to achieve the appropriate spiritual goals:

> Antoninus said to Rebi: The body and the soul can both free themselves from judgment. The body can plead, "The soul has sinned, [the proof being] that from the day it left me I lie like a mute stone in the grave." The soul can say, "The body has sinned, [the proof being] that from the day I departed from it I fly about in the air like a bird." (*Sanhedrin* 91a)

Fly in the air like a bird and…what? It would have been enough for the soul to say that without the body it does not sin. Why did the rabbis compare a bodiless soul to a bird?

Because a bird soars. It can walk on the ground but also fly to the highest of heights. Birds constantly move and do things, and that's what a soul would do if unfettered by a body.

The only problem is, and it is a *major* problem, without a body, a soul can't do anything physical. It can't do any *mitzvos*. It can't learn Torah with *mesiras Nefesh*. In short, a bodiless soul cannot be a partner with God in the fulfillment of the purpose of Creation or be rewarded for it.

This is how the *Gemora* ends:

He (*Rebi*) answered: I will give you a parable. To what may this be compared? To a king who had an excellent garden which contained choice figs, over which he appointed two watchmen, a blind man and a lame man. The lame watchman said to the blind one, "I see choice figs in the garden. Put me on your shoulders and I shall get them, and we will eat them." When the owner of the garden came back and asked them, "What happened to my prize figs?" The blind person answered, "Have I eyes to see them?" The lame one answered, "Have I feet to go to them?" What did the owner do? He put the lame man on the shoulders of the blind man and punished them together. (*Sanhedrin* 91a)

In other words, the body and soul are a unit, divinely paired:

It is a merit, elevation, and great rectification for the soul when it rectifies the body. Both of them were created only for the purpose of the body being rectified by the soul within it. It is also a great elevation for the soul when it completes in this manner what it was sent here to do, so that the two of them can ascend to enjoy and take pleasure from the light of His face[1] itself, *may His name be blessed . . . (Hakdamos uSha'arim, Sha'ar 2, Ch. 2)*

This makes the body more than just extra and un-wanted baggage. The body may be the source of a person's errant behavior, but it is also their ticket to success and fulfillment. We are spiritually chained to our bodies, and this is one "partner" you can't simply run away from. That would be suicide—*literally*.

What if you were chained to someone who was very different from you, who did not share your goals, and who seemed willing to kill you if you went against theirs? Would you capitulate and surrender your values in order to survive, or would you figure out some way to do the impossible and convert them?

One advantage the soul has is God. God never helps the body against the soul, but He does help the soul with the body.[2] He may not stop the body from dragging the soul around everywhere it wants to go if the soul doesn't try to resist. But God will not conspire with the body to undermine the soul if it is doing its best to bring the body over to its way of thinking.

This is the *Avos* and *Imahos*. Moshe *Rabbeinu* was so successful at rectifying his body that, as the *Midrash* says,

---

[1] This refers to a very direct level of light.

[2] As mentioned, God helps a person overcome their *yetzer hara* (*Kiddushin* 30b).

the Angel of Death had a difficult time separating his soul from his body when commanded to do so. But then again, at least the top part of his body had become angelic long before that time.

There are two things to remember. The body itself originates from a higher spiritual source than the soul. It's just that it is more distant from its original source than the soul is from its, allowing the body to be more physical.[3] But it always remains attached to its source and therefore maintains its potential to be extremely *ruchani*—spiritual.

The second thing is that the form of the body we have now was not the one with which man was first created. If the first man were to appear before us today as he existed prior to his sin, we would not be able to see him. His body would be more like a soul than the body we have now.

The physicalization of the body was the result of Adam *HaRishon's* sin. The whole world had been more spiritual than it is now, and was transformed to its current physical state at the same time that Adam's skin went from light to skin.[4] And after history as we know it ends and we reach *Techiyas HaMeisim*, the resurrection of the dead, both man and the world will return to their former spiritual realities.

In the meantime, that is what we are working on each

---

[3] *Hakdamos uSha'arim, Sha'ar* 2, Ch. 1-2.
[4] *Drushei Olam HaTohu, Drush Aitz HaDa'as.*

day of our lives, or least we should be. Every bit of Torah we learn and every *mitzvah* we perform accomplishes this, though we can't necessarily see the results yet. If people could, then they would see the truth of Torah without having worked it out intellectually.

If you want to see a hint to all of this, just look at a *ba'al teshuvah*. It is amazing the extent to which the learning of Torah and the performance of *mitzvos* can refine the body of someone who was once spiritually unrefined. There is humility where once it was lacking, refined speech instead of coarse or even abusive speech, and far more self-discipline when it comes to the demands of their body.

Tzaddikim even seem to have a glow about them, and to exude some kind of *chayn*. They certainly seem to have a presence about them that seems more like a soul than a body. They deny themselves niceties of this world, but not because they impose it upon themselves. Their body is so attuned to their soul that it also lost its desire for them.

Aging people also make this point. A soul never ages but the body does, thanks to the decree of death for eating from the *Aitz HaDa'as Tov v'Ra*, the Tree of Knowledge of Good and Evil. As the body ages it tires and lacks the energy to run after everything it wants. This allows the soul to have more impact on thinking, which is why many become more philosophical as they get older.

This is also why the *halachah* says that we should show respect for an elder, even if they are not a *talmid chacham*, just as we would for a *talmid chacham*. Life has taught them much wisdom, and their aging body is yielding to it.

The trick in life is to already get that wisdom while still young and very much affected by the wants and whims of the body. Every day that the body commands the "ship" is another day that the opportunity to elevate *nitzotzei kedushah* passes a person by. That may not talk to a young body, but it certainly does to an "old" soul.

The *Gemora* makes this point in many places, and there are many verses to this effect. The question is, practically speaking, how do you do it? How do you wake up to the reality of what is really going on in life, and *consciously* live accordingly to maximize the elevation of sparks. How do we make sure we're not someone who will later look back and say, "If only I knew…"

Point of Recognition

here is a story about Saadia *Gaon*[1] that occurred on one of his speaking trips. He used to travel from community to community to answer *halachic* questions and to strengthen the faith of those who came to hear him speak.

On one occasion, the *Gaon* tried to get a room at the local inn, but was told by the innkeeper that his place was filled to capacity on account of the great Saadia *Gaon* who had come to speak. The innkeeper had no idea that he was actually talking to the man himself.

---

[1] Rabbi Saadia *ben* Yosef Al-Fayyumi (882/892 – 942). *Gaon* means "genius."

The *Gaon* said that he didn't need much, just a simple room and bed. The innkeeper, having mercy, told Rav Saadia that he could sleep on the bed in his utility room if he liked. The *Gaon* gratefully accepted the offer and said no more.

The next day the innkeeper went out to hear the great rabbi speak. He nearly had a heart attack once he was able to see that the man sleeping in his utility room was in fact the *Gaon* himself. He could barely contain himself and waited anxiously for the opportunity to profusely apologize for not treating him more respectfully.

When the *Gaon* had finished, the innkeeper quickly made his way to Rav Saadia. He threw himself down at the feet of the rabbi and, crying profusely, he begged for forgiveness for treating him as he had the day before. The man seemed inconsolable.

"But you treated me perfectly fine," the *Gaon* told the man. "The room was just what I wanted."

"No, it was below the dignity of a rabbi of the *Gaon's* stature!" the sobbing man insisted.

Eventually Rav Saadia returned home and to his own *Bais Midrash*. One night however his students heard a man crying outside in the snow, and quickly run out to see if someone needed help. To their shock, it was their rebi, crying and rolling back and forth in the snow.

"Rebi!" they called out, "What is the matter?!"

Rav Saadia recounted the story of the innkeeper and told his *talmidim*, "It later occurred to me that if the innkeeper, who at first thought he had treated me with disrespect only to feel differently upon finding out my true identity, should I not increase my regret for past sins against God, Whom I come to know better each day?"

It's all about recognition, *hakarah* in Hebrew.[2] A situation may remain exactly the same, but if our recognition of what is going on changes, then so will our appreciation of it. That, in turn, will dictate how we respond and to what extent.

It's really quite amazing how even a small piece of information can completely transform a situation. It can prove the innocence of a person previously assumed guilty, it can save a person from making a grave error they were certain to make, or it can help a person to take advantage of an opportunity they never knew existed.

The *Ohr HaChaim HaKadosh* asks why Adam *HaRishon* did not first eat from the *Aitz HaChaim,* which promised eternal life, before eating from the *Aitz HaDa'as,* which led to death. If you plan to eat the poison and live, shouldn't you first take the antidote?

He answers that the *Aitz HaChaim* was actually the trunk of the tree that all the other trees grew off of, including the *Aitz HaDa'as.*[3] But unlike the other "trees" whose

---

[2] The word is also used for *consciousness* today.

[3] As a result of the sin, the branches broke off and became independent trees (*Pri Tzaddik, Tu B'Shevat*).

fruit was *"pleasing to the eyes,"*[4] the fruit of the *Aitz HaChaim* was actually its bark, and did not appeal to the eyes.

Therefore, Adam *HaRishon* could not have known how good the "fruit" of the *Aitz HaChaim* was until he ate from it. As Shlomo *HaMelech* wrote:

It is a tree of life for those who grasp it. (*Mishlei* 3:18)

Only for the person who "grasps" it does it become an *Aitz HaChaim*.

That's how it works. When you learn something new, you become more cognizant of other aspects of life. Some of them might seem trivial at first, but as you learn more about them, their importance becomes more apparent, and this automatically impacts your approach to life. Yes, a little bit of knowledge can be a dangerous thing, but usually only when it isn't followed up with the necessary additional knowledge.

There is no such thing as a happy hypocrite. By virtue of the soul within us, we have a difficult time knowing the truth and living according to the opposite of it. Stronger people admit the truth and adjust their lives accordingly. Weaker people end up doing weird things to avoid change and to suppress their soul's innate sense of honesty, but it always hurts them on some level.

---

[4] *Bereishis* 3:6.

The starting point? One question to ask yourself:

Do I want to be a major player, or a second on the set?

Before you answer, let me recount another story. After World War II was over, certain rabbis went out to try and locate Jewish children left with gentile neighbors to spare them the horrors of the Holocaust. The trouble is that many of them were too young to remember their parents, and some had already been "adopted" by their gentile guardians.

One tactic was to gather suspected Jewish children together, say the "*Shema*" out loud, and look for signs of recognition. On some occasions there were some, and after investigating the history of the child, they were able to confirm the Jewish status of some of the children and return them to their rightful relatives.

Likewise, when you ask yourself, "Do I want to be a major player in God's history?" something inside you might immediately jump up and say, "Yes!" But moments later, another voice might cut in and say, "Are you kidding?! Do you know what that entails? Being only a 'second' has great benefits too..."

It's that first voice you want to pay attention to, the one that showed signs of recognition about what life is really about. That was the soul speaking up and saying, "I don't want to be mediocre. I want to be the greatest me I can possibly be. Let's do the greater thing!" The second is usually the voice of the *yetzer hara*, our bodily instinct to choose comfort over all else.

My *Rosh Yeshivah* used to ask people, "Do you like pleasure?" and of course they would answer, "Yes." So he would say to them, "Come to the *yeshivah* for a couple of weeks and we'll show you how to really get the most pleasure out of life." Knowing that meant possibly having to admit that Torah was from God and true, they usually declined. So the *Rosh Yeshivah* would tell them, "You may like pleasure, but you love comfort more."

It's the soul that loves pleasure, and the body that loves comfort, and often they are not the same thing. We often have to work hard for some of our favorite pleasures, and comfort is usually the result of doing nothing or very little, though we also need some of that occasionally.

What is the greatest pleasure a person can have? Is it the same for everyone? If you compared personal lists of favorite pleasures, there would be some overlap, but differences as well. Number one on one person's list could be number four on another person's list, and number six on another's.

But that's only because most people have not yet experienced the greatest pleasure, or recognized it for what it was if they did. There may not have been much hype or celebration surrounding the moment, which may have been fleeting. And for people who define pleasure as comfort, it might be something they have actually avoided all of their lives.

The greatest pleasure? Personal wholeness.

It's like two wires that are separate from each other. They might be next to each other, above and below one another, but until they are connected to each other, the light they help power cannot shine and illuminate the world.

Likewise, though the body and the soul are in close proximity of one another, they must connect for a person to feel whole…alive…illuminating. While separate from each other they are just two mismatched parts of a whole. But when they come to share one reality, they synergize into a glorious work of God that generates constant energy and elation, something that very, very few people have experienced.

History shows and experience proves that this is never the result of the soul capitulating to the body, but the result of the body succumbing to the leadership of the soul. It would kill the soul to lose its spiritual identity and become like the body, but it would give even more life to the body to become like the soul. The body only thinks it will die from being more spiritual.

But as any *ba'al teshuvah* will tell you, the body learns otherwise as it becomes more learned and increases its awareness of the truth about life. It will reach this point of recognition eventually anyhow, moments before it dies and can't do anything about it other than feel regret. Or it can happen while it is still young enough to switch tracks and become a spark elevator.

The body is a panicker. It looks at every task in terms of the total amount of work it will have to perform to accomplish it. If it is a small amount then it might not complain. But if the effort needed to succeed is large, then it will panic and do whatever it can to avoid involvement. It doesn't seem to realize or appreciate that even the largest problems can be overcome in time and in increments.

Take the spies in Moshe's time, for example. Rather than wait the three days journey to *Eretz Yisroel*, they ran ahead to get a sneak preview of the land and the people living there. But they did it with their current perspective, which lacked the benefit of three days of development.

Consequently, they could not fathom, *with their current mentality*, how they would be able to rise to the task of conquering the 31 kings of Canaan. So they panicked and caused the nation to panic, and it cost them their lives, 39 extra years of exile, and thousands of years more throughout the rest of history.

The truth is, the spies had not been wrong. They had been right that the nation could not, in its current state, conquer the Canaanites and take the land. But God already knew that, which is why He had not planned to bring them there for another three days, another three *crucial* days of spiritual development growth during which they would have *become* ready.

What would have changed during only three days? We'll never know now, but we can assume that it was what was accomplished, at least somewhat, over the next 39 years, more-or-less. I say *somewhat* because, even after the 39 years were over and Yehoshua took the people into the land, it did not end as well as it was supposed to, evident from the exile that followed 850 years later, not to mention the rest of Jewish history.

But had history gone the way it was supposed to have, then divine providence would have done what was necessary to raise the sights of the Jewish people. God would have educated us, one way or another, and increased our level of consciousness and recognition. We would have become aware of things that would have transformed our vision of reality, and taking *Eretz Yisroel* would have appeared vastly different then than it did to the spiritually underdeveloped spies.

It is the essence of *teshuvah* and life. You know when *teshuvah* is a big thing, a *hard* thing? When you know where you have to be, but you don't know how to get there. There is an overwhelming gap between what you ought to feel, and what you presently feel. Why wouldn't the body feel intimidated and want to run the other way?

And yet, how many times have we found ourselves on the other side looking back and wondering, "What was the big deal? What was I so nervous about?" Then you have difficulty feeling currently what you felt back then, before…before you reached your point of recognition.

A good educator knows this. Rather than try to force a student to accept a new way of thinking, they lead them there, one intellectual step after another. They start with one idea the student can grasp, can reach up to, and when they acquire that one, they move on to the next one. Climbing a mountain is just the result of a lot of very small steps upon the mountain side, at the end of which you *find* yourself at the top.

Learning works the same way. When you learn something new and develop a relationship to it, your life will automatically change. It might be imperceptible at first, but as the small changes accumulate with the addition of new information, you just find yourself changed one day.

They have built tunnels through mountains where I live. It is an incredible task to bore through so much rock and then run perfectly paved roads through them. When they start, it seems like it will take forever until they are open for use.

Some of the progress you can see, but a lot of it is hidden from view by the mountain. Even right before it opens, it seems like it will still take considerable time before the work is complete, and you get a little impatient. Once open, it will be a sight to see and road to take.

Then all of a sudden, and quite quickly, the project looks done, and before you know it, cars are using it. There is a sense of marvel at how it is "already" done, seemingly quicker than anticipated by those not involved in its construction.

There is another point to consider in all of this. The *Gemora* says:

[While the fetus is still in the womb] they teach it all of Torah…Once the child is born an angel touches it above the mouth and it forgets all of Torah. (*Niddah* 30b)

Literal or not, the point is the point. The Point of Recognition does not require us to first find the knowledge to achieve that recognition. It is already inside of us on the level of our soul. We just have to become conscious of it, which is what we do through education.

It may look like were pulling down ideas from the outside, but when we "learn" something new, we're really pulling up ideas from the inside, spiritually speaking. Every level of recognition a person can achieve in their lifetime is already inside of them, and the tragedy is that people die leaving most of them undiscovered.

Because the soul has five levels, and the higher the level of soul, the deeper and more profound the knowledge it has access to. Since levels and areas of Torah learning correspond to different levels of soul, accessing levels of the former allows for access to levels of the latter.[5] The sky is not the limit here. Heaven is.

So, the next time you look in the mirror, take note. You appear as you do because of your current point of recognition. How we look on the outside is a reflection of

---

[5] This is the idea of *Pardes*, which is explained in my book, *The Big Picture: Thirty-six Sessions to Intellectual & Spiritual Clarity*.

how we see ourselves on the inside. As you change the latter, the former will automatically change too, perhaps imperceptibly at first, but over time, dramatically.

As you do, you will not appear more like a stranger to yourself, but less. You will seem and feel more fulfilled, because the real "you" is not what you start out as, but what you become over time. And the more you become, the more you you will become. And at some point, you will even find yourself looking back at a younger version of yourself, asking, "How could I have thought I was all I had to be at the time?"

To Be A

his chapter is not for you, at least not *all* of you. It is for your soul, the *essence* of you. It is meant to inspire it to rise up and break out, and to become the hero it was always meant to be.

The hero is embedded in every culture. Somehow, each society has come to realize that some people are extraordinary, that they rise above others in one way or another and contribute to the welfare of the world in a somewhat heroic manner.

Some of their specialness is nurtured. For example, some parents push their children to achieve more than average, and over time it becomes their way of life. Some of the uniqueness is inborn, physical or mental abilities that come at birth and enable a person to accomplish more than those less endowed.

There is a lesser known third category. Some people are not necessarily extraordinary physically or mentally, but are with respect to their will. What they lack in physical and intellectual prowess they make up in will. They are driven to do meaningful things, to make a difference, to have an impact. They may not always know how, but they know that they really *want* to.

It's not the attention that they want. It is not in order to receive some recognition or reward. They just want to do it. It's some kind of inner drive and energy that they did not ask for or create. It's just there, like magna below the earth's surface trying to burst forth.

It has to do with the soul of a person, as do most things. It's just that some people's soul has a say in what they do, because they listen to it. Their body may also have a say, or they would be a *tzaddik*. But it doesn't have most of the say as it has in most people throughout history, going all the way back to Adam and Chava.

In societies in which instinct rules, acting non-instinctually for a greater good makes you a hero. All the hero books and movies paint the same picture, albeit with different colors. The hero does the "noble" thing, another way of saying that they listen to their soul over their body. Special abilities like being able to fly or bend metal with bare hands just makes them more fascinating.

Rebi Akiva could not fly, and he was known for his

physical strength. But when the mighty Romans forbade the teaching of Torah in public, he did it anyway. And after they captured him, they raked his skin with iron combs, but that did not stop him from reciting the *Shema* in its proper time. He died saying the word "*Echad*—One."[1]

Rebi Chanina ben Teradyon met a similar fate, though his means of torture and execution was different. But that did not stop him from reassuring his daughter and students that his death was worth it for the sake of God and Torah. He was so heroic in his final moments that the Roman executioner broke ranks, converted to Judaism on the spot, and then jumped into the fire himself as part of his *teshuvah*.[2]

There are so many stories like these, and all of them are heroic because the soul took priority over the body. Most of them have not ended in tragic death, because it is also heroic when a person gives more *tzedakah* than they feel like giving out of mercy for the recipient. It is also heroic when a person feels like speaking *loshon hara*[3] about someone but keeps quiet instead.

It even feels heroic. People who do the wrong thing feel bad about themself, even if they refuse to acknowledge it. Sometimes they even blame others for how they feel because it is easier to try and change others than change

---

[1] *Brochos* 61b.

[2] *Avodah Zarah* 18a.

[3] Derogatory speech about another.

themself. That is the way of *non*-heroic people.

What is the most *non*-heroic thing a person can do? Be selfish. Even though we can be selfish ourselves, we have little tolerance for it in others. It seems so animalistic and worse, because at least animals have no other choice. For them, it is pure survival instinct, and they have no sense of shame. For us, it is only a *default* instinct, and we *do* have a sense of shame.

At the giving of the Torah at Mt. Sinai, everyone was heroic. How do we know this? Because it says:

They traveled from Refidim and came to the Sinai Desert, and they camped in the desert; they (written: he) camped opposite the mountain. (Shemos 19:2)

He camped opposite the mountain: k'ish echad, b'leiv echad—like a single person with a single heart. (*Rashi*)

It doesn't get anymore *selfless* than this. If you were there at that time, you saw millions of individuals, but you felt like part of a single, cohesive, and unified whole. It was a level of unity unknown to mankind, other than when Adam *HaRishon* was first created. And we haven't known it again since the giving of Torah.

The question is, was it incidental to the giving of Torah, or the basis of it? The fact that it is "only a *Rashi*," would suggest the former. Based upon what has been said to this point, it would have to be the latter. Selflessness is the basis of receiving Torah in any generation, and to the extent that a person is selfless is the extent to which they will personally "receive" Torah.

And implement it too. Learning Torah promotes selflessness, and the *mitzvos* provide opportunities to be it. If one's learning of Torah does not make them increasingly less selfish, then they are not truly learning Torah. This will show up in the way they do their *mitzvos* with only half a heart. There's nothing heroic about that.

The soul is innately selfless. It doesn't have a selfish bone anywhere. It doesn't have any bones at all. Being completely spiritual it cannot want the wrong thing. It's greatest pleasure is being part of the whole, which is really God Himself. All of Creation exists within Him so He is the whole thing.

Selfishness belongs to the body. It was built to look out for itself so it can survive, and with needs so it can be used to accomplish things in life. For example, if it didn't need food, the soul would have a difficult time getting the body to eat so it can make *brochos*. If it didn't like pleasure, *oneg* on *Shabbos* would not be possible as a *mitzvah*. It just lacks the *seichel*, which belongs to the soul, to know how much, when, and for what.

This is why inside everyone is a hero looking to get out. Even the most selfish person has a soul, and that soul has to be selfless. They're only selfish because they have fallen prey to bodily instinct, and lack the understanding for why they should rise above and break free. The hero inside is captive under layers of physical parts and sensations.

But we have all had those moments in life when something very big and awesome has happened that neutralized the body long enough to allow the soul to call out for help. And in that moment we sense another level to ourselves, a far more inspiring and exciting level. Amazingly, as fleeting as it may be, it is the most we actually feel ourselves, leaving us longing for more of it after it is gone.

That's the beautiful thing about it. It is already there in the form of a soul. We don't have to create a sense of hero, we just have to reveal it. We just have to peel away the layers of bodily instinct and selfishness and reveal our inner selflessness. We don't have to become heroic. We just have to be the hero we innately are.

We learn Torah and do *mitzvos* to do that.

That's not the end of the story. On the contrary, it is just the beginning of it. The selfless person doesn't just revel in their increased humility and care for the bigger picture. They become fired up to make a difference, as big a difference as possible…for all the right reasons.

After all, all this drive for fame and power really comes from the same place, the need to make a difference, from a need to feel meaningful. But any soul drive filtered through the body will end up being perverted, and that always leads to some form of abuse. Why we do something can be just as important, and often more important, than what we do.

Because that is what pulls the sparks away from the *Klipos* the most, as it says:

The sacrifices of God are a broken spirit… (Tehillim 51:17)

That was what the sacrifices were for, to release *nitzotzei kedushah* back to their sources above. Wood was burned, salt was used, animals were sacrificed, and humans were officiating. All four levels of existence were used, mineral, vegetation, animal, and human, to rectify Creation and make all of it holier.

But the key ingredient? Sincerity. As Shmuel *HaNavi* told Shaul *HaMelech*:

Has God (as much) desire in burnt offerings and peace offerings, as in obeying the voice of God? To obey is better than a peace offering, to listen (is better) than the fat of rams. (1 Shmuel 15:22)

To be great for the wrong reasons is to not be great. You can fool others, but you cannot fool your soul and you certainly cannot fool God. It's going to hurt on some level, reduce their sense of personal completion. It's like working hard to accumulate pretend money knowing that it is really worthless in everyday life.

But if people don't know better, that is what they will do. If they don't understand what life is about, that is the path they will follow. Eventually an entire society will be built upon these ideas and values, as it has been, and people won't even question it. They'll just assume that it is the only way to live.

To lock it in, the *yetzer hara* will offer alternative sources of pleasure and come up with all kinds of distractions. You can always tell what kind of society it is by how much people spend on trivial things just to enhance their "quality" of life, just to feel alive.

We all need food, clothing, and even a little entertainment now and then. But when such things become extreme, it is a sign that people look outside for happiness, not inside. It means their inner hero is so suppressed as to feel non-existent.

But because we get glimpses of it, some people take note of it. They write about it, and when people read about it, it touches something deep inside. There is a connection that often results in a burst of inspiration to be better, more noble. A whole industry has been built around the idea of a hero, but it is considered more fantasy than reality.

Part of the reason is because people don't really know what's involved. Instead they paint pictures of people with superpowers that none of us have. They don't focus on the "superpower" that we do have, and what we can do with it in order to be a hero in the true and ultimate sense.

That's why *tzaddikim* don't get as much attention, if any at all, as the people with higher profiles. All the admiration and adulation that people show to movie stars and wealthy people, in an ideal world, would instead go to the real heroes of society, the people most responsible for elevating holy sparks out of the *Klipos* and rectifying the world for all of us.

Ever since Adam and Chava sinned and were expelled from the Garden, mankind has struggled with the *yetzer hara,* with only a limited amount of victories. For the most part, the *yetzer hara* has won the battle either completely or in part. Empires have come and gone, but the yetzer hara has maintained its control over mankind the entire time and will until *Moshiach* finally subdues it for good.

But happy is the person who is able to stand apart from the billions that haven't. *Truly* happy. In fact, as most people pursue joy in life, they tend to overlook the best place to find it. That important discussion is the next chapter.

ovid *HaMelech* wrote, *"Serve God in joy."*[1] On one hand, this seems like the most obvious thing in the world. Perhaps he felt the need to say this because he had so much *tzuris*[2] throughout his life. Perhaps he was inspired by what God said:

> *All these curses will befall you, pursuing you and overtaking you to destroy you because you did not obey God, your God, to observe His commandments and statutes which He commanded you. And they*

---

[1] *Tehillim* 100:2.

[2] *Yiddish* for *yesurim*—suffering.

will be as a sign and a wonder, upon you and your offspring, forever, because you did not serve God, your God, in joy and with gladness of heart, when [you had an] abundance of everything. (Devarim 28:45-47)

On the other hand, if we ask ourselves, "How much joy did we get from our *mitzvos* today, or yesterday, or the day before that, etc.?" what would we answer? A *lot*? An *average* amount? Very *little*? That last *brochah* you said…did you enjoy making it? Do you still feel the pleasure?

Non-religious people are intimidated by *mitzvos* because they don't think they'll enjoy them. But why should they, if we who do them don't look as if they're the greatest gift we could have ever received? Clearly Dovid *HaMelech* knew exactly what he was doing when he told all of us to serve God with joy.

The problem is that people confuse *oneg* for *simchah*. *Oneg* is pleasure, usually *physical* pleasure. There is a *mitzvah* of *oneg Shabbos*, to have pleasure on *Shabbos*, so we make a point of eating foods and wearing clothes that we *physically* enjoy.

Simchah is different. For example, we eat meat and drink wine on *Yom Tov* because it is a time for *simchah*. But the meat and the wine, unlike with respect to *Shabbos*, are not because they provide *oneg* (although that doesn't hurt). It is because they *remind* us of how we used to go up to the Temple on the *Shalosh Regalim—Pesach, Shavu-*

os, and *Succos*—and eat from the meat of the sacrifices that we brought up, and of the wine libations we brought as well to be offered on the altar. That *intellectual* connection generates the *simchah*.

This is why *Succos* is called *zman simchasaynu*, the time of our joy, more than the other *chagim*. Even though *Pesach* was freedom from the spiritually limiting Egyptian mentality, we mostly identify it with physical freedom. So it is called, *zman cheirusaynu*—the time of our freedom.

And though *Shavuos* is *zman Torahsaynu*, the time of receiving our Torah, we have to be told to derive *simchah* from doing *mitzvos*. And not everyone loves learning Torah, or learning it *lishmah*, altruistically. It can even be frustrating to learn at times, which is why so many leave it for other activities instead.

But *Succos* comes after *Yom Kippur*, the holiday of *binah*—understanding. It is the holiday on which we reach such a level of intellectual and spiritual clarity that we are compared to angels. It is the holiday during which we tell our bodies to take a backseat to the soul. That is the wonderful feeling we have after a "good" *Yom Kippur*, the joy that comes from a liberated soul.

We carry this reality all the way to *Succos,* whose walls are compared to a body, and the person inside it, to a soul. Just as the walls of a *succah* are only temporary while the person inside it is not, likewise a body is only temporary while the soul it hosts will live beyond it.

And the *arba minim* that we take and wave on the

chag, the *lulav*, *esrog*, *hadassim*, and *aravos*, all symbolize different character traits, some that we should adopt and some that we should avoid. It's all about giving the soul the upper hand the rest of the year…and living with joy.

So when God said, *"because you did not serve God, your God, in joy,"* He was saying that we did not serve Him with our souls. Had we, then we would have exuded joy everyday, and that would have also shown that we knew and appreciated that the *mitzvos* were for us, not for God:

> Rebi Chananya *ben* Akashya said: "The Holy One, Blessed is He, wished to make the Jewish people meritorious. Therefore He gave them Torah and *mitzvos* in abundant measure…" (*Makkos* 23b)

But when it comes to *simchah*, *soul* is too general a term, because joy is not relevant to the entire soul. Because, there are five levels of soul, and joy is not relevant to all of them, and it is important to know why.

The five levels of soul are, from the bottom up: *Nefesh, Ruach, Neshamah, Chayah*, and *Yechidah*.[3] We always have all five because they are the means by which the light of God comes down to us so that we can live and accomplish. It's just that we can't access the two upper levels since Adam *HaRishon* lost them after sinning.

Therefore, when a person comes into the world,

---

[3] *Sha'ar HaGilgulim*, Introduction 1.

which is only for the sake of *tikun*, they are here to rectify either their *Nefesh, Ruach*, or *Neshamah*, but in that order. We won't regain access to *Chayah* and *Yechidah* until well into the future.

It is possible to rectify all three levels in a single lifetime, but only the first time. If during the first incarnation a person did not rectify their *Nefesh, Ruach*, and *Neshamah*, they cannot rectify more than one level in a single lifetime. When they finish one, they will have to die and reincarnate to work on their next level.[4]

For example, If a person only rectified 60 percent of their *Nefesh* before dying, they will have to reincarnate to rectify the remaining 40 percent. If they do that in their second incarnation, they will have to die and reincarnate again to gain access to the level of *Ruach* to rectify that, whether they are young or old.

If they happened to rectify their *Ruach* all in one lifetime, they will still have to die to gain access to their *Neshamah* to work on that, since it is not their first lifetime. And they will keep reincarnating until they have rectified all three levels of *Nefesh, Ruach*, and *Neshamah*, or history runs out of time. What is left over at that point will have to be dealt with in the next world.

Where it gets interesting is in *Techiyas HaMeisim*, the period of resurrecting the dead. Since a single soul could have lived in many bodies throughout its course of person-

---

[4] *Sha'ar HaGilgulim.*

al rectification, the question becomes, which body is resurrected? The answer is, basically all of them.[5] Each body will
resurrect with the percentage of soul that was rectified during its lifetimes.

Therefore, the body that rectified only 60 percent of
the *Nefesh* will return with that 60 percent of the *Nefesh*,
and nothing else. The next body that rectified the remaining 40 percent of the *Nefesh* will resurrect with that 40 percent, and nothing else. The body that rectified the *Ruach*
will come back with the *Ruach*, etc.

Eventually all the parts of the soul will merge once
again in the World-to-Come, as will everything else as Creation heads in the direction of sublime unification with its
Creator. But at least for the period of *Techiyas HaMeisim*,
"our" multiple bodies will enjoy multiple parts of our soul.

But, the *Arizal* explained, the actual pleasure from
the soul will only be for the bodies that rectified the *Ruach*
up. The ones with only the *Nefesh* will not have much pleasure after resurrection because the *Nefesh*, a level of soul
we share with animals, is just not that spiritually exciting a
level of soul. And, as the *Arizal* says, few people make it
past the level of *Nefesh*.[6]

Not because they *can't*, but because they *won't*. They

---

[5] The only body not resurrected is the one used to commit a sin for
which the punishment is *kares*—excision (*Sha'ar HaGilgulim*, Introduction 30).

[6] *Sha'ar HaGilgulim*, Introduction 1.

won't learn Torah because they do not believe in it. Or, if they believe in Torah, they won't learn it on the level necessary to access higher levels of soul. They accept their current level of spiritual living as sufficient, and aren't curious enough to find out if it isn't.

How can you even know which level of soul you are on? Without prophecy, you can't with any certainty. But there are some signs that can provide a good indication of which level of soul a person is currently accessing. Taking note of these is the first step to personal rectification and greater joy in life.

It all comes down to how spiritually refined a life you live. As a person grows in levels of soul, they become increasingly spiritually refined. Material pleasures they once thought they could not live without become unimportant and superfluous. Spiritual pleasures however gain importance and become more of a priority as a person gains access to higher levels of soul.

The best part though is an enhanced relationship with God. There are radio signals bouncing around all around us, but we are oblivious to them without the proper device to receive and interpret them for us. Likewise, God is always around us, but without sufficient spiritual sensitivity, we can't pick up His "frequency." That becomes easier as a person accesses higher levels of soul.

What about the body? Does an advancing soul leave a spiritually stagnating body behind? It can. But more often than not, the body is influenced by the growth of the soul, at first reluctantly, but eventually with joy. Once the body has had a good taste of the joy of the soul, it realizes how wrong it previously was about spiritual pleasure. Whereas once it was relentless about material pleasures, it learns to be that way about spiritual ones instead, as any *ba'al teshuvah* will tell you.

Until that time, if a person ever reaches it, the body can be the greatest obstacle to true joy in life. Spiritually uneducated and physically unbridled, it can be a powerful force in the way of the soul and its ambitions. It has no idea how much joy it is sacrificing on the altar of physical gratification. It has no clue *what is really going on.*

The *good* news is that there is still time to change.

The *bad* news is that there is not much left.

We're at one of those points in history where our minds and emotions differ about what is happening. History has already lived 5783 years out of its allotted 6,000. Of the remaining 217 years, the *Zohar* says either 210 or 214 of them are for *Techiyas HaMeisim,* a Messianic period of history.[7] That leaves either three or seven years of free will history to make the necessary changes, certainly not enough time to reincarnate and do anything significant.

But when we look around at the world, as different and distant from Torah as it has become, we still have a

---

[7] *Sanhedrin* 97a. Read my books, *Talking About the End of Days* and *Estimated Time of Arrival* for all the other relevant sources and background information.

hard time believing that we're actually at the end. Getting close to it, for sure, *but at it…?* But then again, have we ever been good at recognizing the end of anything? Certainly not on a national scale.

That's very different once you know what is *really* going on in history. It makes the end so much more obvious because it translates the events of the day into a process of elevating holy sparks and rectifying Creation. And just like a person shows signs of aging before they actually get there, and a car will drop off in efficiency as it starts to wear down, Creation acts similarly. *Breaking news is actually "breaking" news.*

There are almost eight billion people in the world today, and the vast majority are busy doing one thing or another. There are the "heroes" of society, and the opposite. There are the rich and famous, and the poor and unknown, and everyone is distracted by something.

Amidst all of that is one person whom God has chosen to be *Moshiach,* the savior of the Jewish people and all mankind. He has been destined to come since Creation, and though he *supposedly* could have come earlier, God knew from the start that he would not be ready to come until now. He may not yet know that he is that chosen one, but it would not take much time to let him know, because he was born ready.

And at that moment, at that *moment* of moments, when God says, "Now," he will emerge onto the world scene which will change rapidly because he has been revealed. There will be those who will fight him to maintain the "status quo," but it will be futile. No one can fight the divine plan for history.

His arrival will turn history on its head. What was up before will all of a sudden be down, and vice-versa. It will pull open the "top" of Creation and reveal for the first time its inner workings. We will be in awe from what we will see, from finally seeing what was really going on the entire time throughout history.

For so many, it will be a repeat of Yosef's brothers after he revealed his true identity to them.[8] They were shocked to the point of debilitation. They couldn't move or speak as they took in what the truth of their brother's revelation meant regarding the last 22 years of their lives, not to mention their *entire* lives.

People have made many wrong assumptions about what life is about, and have invested their entire lives based upon those faulty assumptions. Even many who believe in God and live by Torah will be very "surprised" to see what they could have actually been doing when they learned Torah and performed *mitzvos,* and what they did instead.

Many will not. Not everyone is meant to have a dramatic impact on history. Not everyone has the capacity to make a big difference. Yosef's brothers had their reaction because they were great people who were destined for great things. That's why they did what they did, and were

---

[8] *Bereishis* 45:3.

so pained by their error.

Lesser people would have simply apologized for their mistake. They probably would not have done what the brothers did in the first place, choosing instead to ignore Yosef and work around him. Lacking any real desire to fix the world as a partner of God, they would have taken the path of least resistance, and so many have throughout history.

But for the rare few who want to be a hero of God for the right reasons, who want to be movers-and-shakers of the right things…movers of *nitzotzei kedushah* out of the *Klipos*…shakers of the sparks to clean them from impurity…it is time. It is time to see clearly what is really going on, and to fall-in with the program, *God's* program.

It is your *true* destiny.

Other Books

If Only I Were Wealthy
If Only I Could See the Forest,
If Only Great Was Greater
Changes that Last Forever
Bereishis: A Beginning With No End
Redemption to Redemption,
The Big Picture
Perceptions
Talking About The End-of-Days,
Talking About *Eretz Yisroel*
The Physics of *Kabbalah*
Be Positive
Geulah b'Rachamim
God.calm
Sha'ar HaGilgulim (Translation)
Just Passing Through
On The Same Page
The Equation of Life
No Such Victim
Survival in 10 Easy Steps
Not Just Another Scenario 2
All In Your Mind
The Light of 36

Drowning in *Pshat*
Shas Man
The Mystery of Jewish History
Survival Guide For the End-of-Days
Deeper Perceptions
Chanukah Lite
Hitchhiker's Guide to Armageddon
Purim Lite
Pesach Lite
The Torah Empowerment Seminar
The Fabric of Reality
Fundamentals of Reincarnation
Reincarnation Clarified
All About Energy
What Goes Around
The God Experience, Part 1
What in Heaven
The God Experience, Part 2
The God Experience, Part 3
It's About Time
Need to Know
Perceptions, Volume 2
Once Revealed, Twice Concealed

All books are usually available in Kindle, Paperback, and PDF formats, and some in Hardcover as well. The PDF books can be purchased through the Thirtysix.org online bookstore, and the other books are available through Amazon.com. For additional information, write to:

pinchasw@thirtysix.org

www.ingramcontent.com/pod-product-compliance
Lightning Source LLC
Chambersburg PA
CBHW071329140726
47996CB00005B/1893